Sister of the Solid Rock

Edna Mae Barnes Martin and the East Side Christian Center

Sister of the Solid Rock

Edna Mae Barnes Martin and the East Side Christian Center

By Wilma Rugh Taylor

INDIANA HISTORICAL SOCIETY PRESS
INDIANAPOLIS 2002

This book is a publication of the
Indiana Historical Society Press
450 West Ohio Street
Indianapolis, Indiana 46202-3269 USA
www.indianahistory.org
Telephone orders 1-800-447-1830
Fax orders 317-234-0562
Orders by E-mail shop.indianahistory.org

The paper in this publication meets the minimum requirements of American National Standard for Information Sciences—Permanence of Paper for Printed Library Materials, ANSI Z39.48—1984. ∞

Library of Congress Cataloging-in-Publication Data

Taylor, Wilma Rugh.
    Sister of the solid rock: Edna Mae Barnes Martin and the East Side Christian Center / by Wilma Rugh Taylor.
      p. cm.
    Includes bibliographical references and index.
    ISBN 0-87195-161-4 (alk. paper)
      1. Martin, Edna Mae Barnes, 1897-1974. 2. Baptists—Indiana—Biography. 3. East Side Christian Center. I. Title.

BX6495.M327 T39 2002
286'.1'092—dc21
[B]   2002068878

This book is dedicated to the memory of

Edna Mae Barnes Martin,

whose story of courage and grace is told in this book,

and to

Edna Mae Overman Rugh,

my mother,
who like Edna Mae Barnes Martin
shared the story of God's love to the homeless
and hopeless and to the throngs of women
who came to her Bible classes across
the city of Indianapolis in the 1930s and 1940s.

Therefore everyone who hears these words of mine, and
acts upon them, may be compared to a wise man,
who built his house upon the rock.

And the rain descended, and the floods came, and
the winds blew, and burst against that house; and yet
it did not fall, for it had been founded upon the rock.

And everyone who hears these words of mine, and
does not act upon them, will be like a foolish man,
who built his house upon the sand.

And the rain descended, and the floods came, and
the winds blew, and burst against that house; and it fell,
and great was its fall.

Matthew 7:24–27

"On Christ the Solid Rock I Stand,
All Other Ground Is Sinking Sand,
All Other Ground Is Sinking Sand."

Hymn "The Solid Rock"

Table of Contents

Foreword

Edna Mae Barnes Martin's biography provides its reader with a unique view of the culture and aspirations of blacks who migrated from Kentucky and Tennessee to Indiana, and especially Indianapolis, the state's capital, during the first three quarters of the twentieth century. Edna Mae Barnes's family was a part of the first wave of African Americans to make this trek during the first decade of the twentieth century. In 1896 Edna's parents, William Barnes, who was born on a farm in Crittenden County, Kentucky, in 1872, and Lemah Jones Barnes, who was born on a farm in Livingston County, Kentucky, in 1877, and their one-year-old-son Duke left their home in Paducah, Kentucky, and embarked on a five-year journey through southern Indiana in their quest of the American Dream. Their first stop was Marrs Township, a farming community located just across the Ohio River near Mount Vernon, where Edna was born on 25 November 1897. The second stop was Baptisttown, Evansville's African-American community, where Lucille, a second daughter, was born in 1900. The family reached its ultimate destination of Indianapolis in 1901. Here their last four children, Thelma, Marie, Harold, and Arletta, were born.

The Barnes family, like many of the other African Americans who migrated from Kentucky and Tennessee to Indianapolis, carried much agrarian cultural baggage with them. William and Lemah Barnes, like many of their fellow migrants, had been born and raised on African-American farms, where their lives had been atuned to the rhythm cycle of the four seasons: plant in the spring, cultivate in the summer, harvest in the fall, and refurbish the homestead during the winter. This annual life cycle also instilled certain community values that Edna would embrace and later use during the course of her career. For example, the value of cooperation was taught every fall when the area farmers would go from farm to farm and help their neighbors kill and preserve their meat for the winter. The women of these farming communities demonstrated the value of thrift to their daughters during the winter quilting bees, where they would gather in a neighbor's homestead and fash- ion the scraps of cloth and worn-out items of clothing that they had saved during the year into quilts. Summer revivals and baptisms were annual community evangelical rituals that reaf- firmed traditional Christian values and beliefs that the Barnes family and countless other African-American migrants from Kentucky and Tennessee brought with them to Indianapolis. Among these basic tenets are these: the teachings of the Bible are infallible; salvation can only be achieved through personal acceptance of Jesus Christ as your Lord and Savior; all Christians are obligated to engage in public service to help their less fortunate brothers and sisters; and God, not mankind, controls the affairs of the world—those who submit to God's will succeed, those who resist His call fail. These cul- tural values are evident throughout the life and legacy of Edna Mae Barnes Martin.

From 1900 to 1940, the period prior to Edna's public service career, Indianapolis race relations were quite hostile. Perhaps the nadir of this period was the decade of the 1920s, which wit- nessed the rise of the Ku Klux Klan in civic and governmental circles, especially the police department; the enactment of zoning ordinances by white homeowners to keep African-American families from moving into their neighborhoods; and the bombing of John B. Johnson's home during the summer of 1924. There was also de facto segregation in the public school system. Edna's two children attended the segregated Booker T. Washington Junior High School during the 1930s.

But, in addition to these racial shortcomings, Indianapolis was also the home of many racially progressive institutions and individuals who played a major role in Edna's legacy of public service. She was able to grow her East Side Christian Center by forging valuable interracial alliances with such philanthropists as Edith Stokely Moore, the daughter of the founder of the Stokely Brothers Company; John S. Lynn, the director of the Eli Lilly Foundation; countless white women missionaries in such neighboring towns as Warren, Scottsburg, Dana, Milan, Walden, Sardinia, Petersburg, Boggstown, Washington, and Franklin; and the American Baptist Home Mission Society. These individuals and their philanthropic institutions provided the lion's share of the financial support for Edna's East Side Christian Center.

Indianapolis's African-American community, on the other hand, gave Edna the priceless gifts of self-respect, racial pride, and a burning personal commitment to public service for less fortunate members of the community. For example, an Indianapolis Branch of the National Association for the Advancement of Colored People was founded in 1909; one year later Madam C. J. Walker moved her million-dollar hair production company to Indianapolis. During the 1920s the Senate Avenue YMCA held monthly "Monster Meetings," whose 1925 list of keynote speakers included such national African-American leaders as W. E. B. DuBois of the NAACP. In 1926 the city's African-American citizens were successful in their efforts to have the Indianapolis Public School system name their new high school in honor of Crispus Attucks, an African-American patriot and the nation's first martyr for freedom. In 1932 attorney Henry J. Richardson, Jr., became the first African American elected to the Indiana General Assembly. Literacy was greatly valued in this community. Two African-American newspapers, the *Indianapolis Recorder* and the *Indianapolis Freeman*, were published weekly, keeping their readers abreast of the latest news that impacted upon the African-American community.

It was within this nurturing environment that Edna, the idealist young woman, developed into Edna Mae Barnes Martin, the founder and director of the East Side Christian Center. In 1909 she enrolled in Public School Number 24 and was certainly influenced by the positive role model image presented by her African-American principal Mary Ellen Cable, who was a leader in the racially progressive Woman's Improvement Club and a graduate of Indiana University. In 1914, at the age of seventeen, Edna joined Mount Zion Missionary Baptist Church, where she became active in the church's Lott Carey Missionary Society and met her future husband Earl Martin. Seven years later, on 12 September 1921, they were married. A daughter, Doris Lillian, and a son, Earl William, Jr., were born to this union in 1922 and 1924, respectively. Doris Lillian's death from appendicitis in 1937 left Edna in a state of deep depression, from which she did not fully recover until her twentieth wedding anniversary, when she had the epiphany to start a day care center for the children of working mothers in the city's east side. Edna's public service mission, like her parents' migration to Indianapolis, experienced several stops along the way. Her first site was a one-room day care center in an apartment building at 1475 Roosevelt Avenue; three years later she established the East Side Christian Center in "a three-room shotgun house at 1519 Martindale," which has since been renamed Dr. Andrew Brown Avenue. In 1949 the Center purchased a site at 1537 North Arsenal Avenue, just behind the old Martindale location; on 20 June 1965 a new Caroline Avenue building was dedicated. In 1970 the Lilly Foundation gave the Center an $80,000 grant to purchase an old warehouse on Roosevelt Avenue and convert it into the Soul Ark, a much-needed boys club.

When she died on 25 May 1974 Edna left the rich legacy of a Center that now bears her name and provides services ranging from food distribution to parolee supervision. The Center began in 1941 with two young sisters and a meager budget of $14.00 per month rent and expanded to a clientele of more than five thousand persons per month with an annual operating budget of $78,504.00 by 1970. On 6 June 1965 Franklin College recognized Edna's legacy by awarding her a Doctorate of Humane Letters. In 1972 the Associated Colleges of Indiana inducted Edna into the Indiana Academy, along with such Hoosier notables as Eugene S. Pulliam, publisher of the *Indianapolis Star/News*; Richard G. Lugar, Indianapolis mayor; and Eli Lilly, chairman of the board of Eli Lilly and Company. But, as important as these honors were, Edna found her greatest satisfaction in doing the will of God as it led her missionary efforts among the citizens on the east side of Indianapolis—a lesson that she learned well within her church and Indianapolis's African-American community.

William H. Wiggins, Jr.
Professor of Afro-American Studies
Indiana University, Bloomington

Preface

It was just a fourteen-dollar-per-month room in a run-down apartment house in one of Indianapolis's most economically distressed neighborhoods. What in the 1941 world did a forty-four-year-old wife and mother with a comfortable home of her own, busy in her church and community on the other side of town, want with such a place?

It seemed simple to Edna Mae Barnes Martin. She was fired up after attending spirited meetings held by the Indianapolis All Baptist Fellowship, a consortium of ninety-two black and white churches determined to do more than "just talk" about racial polarization and material and spiritual poverty. She had read with alarm the Indianapolis Church Federation's reports about the escalating crime rate among the youth of the east side district now known as Martindale, a neighborhood first settled by African Americans in 1878,[1] and she determined to do something about it.

Indiana historian Emma Lou Thornbrough, in "The History of Black Women in Indiana," writes that "the role of women in history has been traditionally regarded as passive and supportive."[2] That was especially true of black women. There was nothing passive about Edna Mae Barnes Martin. In the midst of the misery of an Indianapolis ghetto, she would reach out and hug children that no one else wanted to touch. She would radiate light and hope for those little ones and their families, and, in doing so, generate more than a bit of controversy. Edna Martin's ways were not always the ways of those who operated in her quiet but confident sphere of endeavor. Some would come to call her style "old-fashioned stubbornness," but to Edna it was simply steadfastness.

She was an activist in the mode of a Mother Teresa. Her stance did not come from the teachings of the traditional male-dominated church. She did not accept the ideologies of social reformers or the rhetoric of militant organizers, even nonviolent ones. Edna's manifesto was more in the manner of the parables of the Good Samaritan, the Prodigal Son, and the Lost Sheep. To Edna Martin, the plain, unpoliticized Gospel of Jesus Christ was the only way to change lives and neighborhoods. As the old hymn proclaims, "All other ground is sinking sand."

For over thirty years she molded the lives of hundreds of Indianapolis children, reformed so-called unredeemable boys, trained girls to be competent women, clothed and fed multitudes, and found jobs for the unemployed. She changed the racial perceptions of hundreds of white citizens and raised funds from private individuals and great foundations.

She would exasperate, at times, both black and white church and community movers and shakers. Yet, she would also captivate congregations from the rural communities of southern Indiana to the lofty spires of New York City's historic Riverside Church. The house that Edna Martin would build upon her rock and resolve would grow from a tiny room jammed with tattered children to a Christian center named in her honor.

Acknowledgments

At the heart of Edna Martin's mission in life was her love for children. It is my desire that this book will result in increased devotion to the children and staff of the Edna Martin Christian Center.

In 1990 the Indiana Historical Society gave a grant to the Edna Martin Christian Center Board to pursue this biography. Two other researchers, Karen Bridges and Gwendolyn Crenshaw, contributed to this project. I am indebted to them for their invaluable oral histories of the Martin family and of others at the heart of the Center.

When Rev. Marsha Bridwell McDaniel and the Edna Martin Christian Center Board asked if I would finish this work, I was pleased that I would have the opportunity to bring Edna Martin's story to a broader audience. The Edna Martin Christian Center Board, Dr. Lawrence Lindley, director, and Evelyn Stewart, program director, has been faithful in its support.

It was on the anniversary of Edna's death, 25 May 2001, that I spoke with two of Edna's grandchildren, James Robert Martin and Brenda Martin Wilcox. They were thrilled that the Indiana Historical Society wanted to publish their grandmother's story.

I am grateful for the shared memories of all the family members.

Pastors Jon Carlstrom, Paul Crafton and his wife Susie Breedlove Crafton, Louis Nelson, L. Eugene Ton, Dallas J. West, Orville Sutton, Ron Kerr, George Kimsey, Richard Padrick, and Frank Alexander helped me understand the broader impact of Edna's contributions.

Effie Behrens, widow of Dr. Otto Behrens, one of the early board members, and Rosa Lee Brown, widow of Dr. Andrew J. Brown, esteemed longtime pastor of St. John Missionary Baptist Church and civil rights activist, shared their memories of Edna, as did Mildred Majors, a Center volunteer and mother. Celestine D. Pettrie, Edna's Indianapolis Avenue neighbor, who submitted Edna's story to the Queen for a Day radio program (which was not accepted), was thankful that now "the world would know what a wonderful woman Edna was."

Dr. Edwin S. Gaustad, professor emeritus of history at the University of California, Riverside, and Dr. Eldon Ernst, professor emeritus of American church history, American Baptist Seminary of the West, both premier historians, are my role models. I could only aspire to make the mark in Baptist history that they have made with their numerous works.

I am so grateful to John Lynn, Edna's friend and benefactor from the Lilly Endowment Foundation, who recalled the qualities that caused him to support the Center and further Edna's vision.

Wilma L. Gibbs, archivist, African-American history, Indiana Historical Society, and Etan Diamond and The Polis Center Project on Religion and Urban Culture contributed valuable sources and inspiration.

The staffs of the American Baptist Churches of Indiana and Kentucky and the American Baptist Churches of Greater Indianapolis gave generous assistance, as did Mary Alice Medlicott, archivist, Indiana Baptist Collection, Franklin College, and Lynne Schuetz, the Johnson County Historical Society. My dear friends, Betty Layton, archivist, and Deborah B. Van Broekhoven, executive director, American Baptist

Historical Society at Valley Forge, Pennsylvania, as always uplifted me in the project.

Dr. Dadashinarehema (Jeanette) Jones and Jo Diane Westmoreland Ivey shared vivid images of themselves as children sitting at the feet of Edna Martin. Carrie Bell Brown, former director of the Dayton (Ohio) Christian Center, recalled "Saint Edna."

For his conviction that Edna Martin's life would shed invaluable historical and cultural insights into Indiana history from 1900 to 1971, I am grateful to Dr. William H. Wiggins, Jr., Department of Afro-American Studies, Indiana University, who so kindly offered to write the foreword for this book.

Doris Rugh, my sister-in-law who passed away before the book was completed, and my beloved Harriet Dowdy, whose husband was a pastor at Woodruff Place Baptist Church, mentored me through *This Train Is Bound for Glory* and this book.

In spring 1999 I discussed with Robert M. Taylor, Jr., director of education for the Indiana Historical Society, the writing of this book. It was his hope that the Society would publish Edna's story, which had been part of his own denominational experience. In October 1999 he passed away unexpectedly. This book honors his memory.

I am indebted for the confidence of Thomas A. Mason, vice president of publications, Indiana Historical Society, and to the wise and gentle guidance of senior editor Paula Corpuz. Special thanks go to editors Judith Q. McMullen, whose gracious manner made the process so pleasant, and Kathleen M. Breen, who aided in the onerous task of checking all my sources.

The memory of Rev. Ralph Beaty and his radiant devotion to the ministry of the Edna Martin Christian Center was my constant inspiration.

Barbara Smith, author and my writing instructor at the Green Lake Writers' Conference, kindly provided editing assistance and encouragement for this project.

My children and their precious families always are at the heart of my writing projects. Because of them, I have the desire to tell stories of God's love and grace so that they too will become storytellers for Him.

In all of my creative efforts, my dearest friend and supporter is my husband Norman. He knew this was a special project for me.

I have tried my best to tell Edna's story, for like Edna, I believe in the edict of Ecclesiastes 5:4: "When you vow to God, do not delay paying it; for he has no pleasure in fools." Like Edna Mae Barnes Martin, and like my mother Edna Mae Overman Rugh, I, too, stand on the Solid Rock—for "all other ground is sinking sand."

CHAPTER ONE

From Kentucky Roots to Indiana River Towns

Similar to many members of the Indianapolis black community around the turn of the century, Edna Mae Barnes Martin's father, William Barnes, and mother, Lemah Jones Barnes, were born in Kentucky and journeyed to Indiana via Ohio River towns. They arrived in Mt. Vernon, Indiana, in 1897 and were part of a migration that preceded the Great Migration movement—the greatest surge of African Americans from the South to the North in search of equality and opportunity that began in 1910. In 1890, of the 90 percent of the black population in America who resided in the South, more than 80 percent lived in the rural "black belt" counties. The vast majority, like Edna's parents, were farmers, sharecroppers or tenants, and unskilled workers.[1]

In his study of Evansville, Indiana's major river town, Darrel E. Bigham wrote, "The deterioration of the quality of life of southern blacks in the two decades prior to World War I, coupled with a labor shortage in the industrial North, stimulated the migration. The rise of Jim Crow, the disfranchisement of black voters, and the spread of lynchings and other mob violence against blacks also provided strong impetus for individuals and families to move. Widespread flooding and the infestation of cotton by the boll weevil created additional economic woes in the rural South."[2]

William Barnes was born in 1872 in Crittenden County, Kentucky, a county bordering the Ohio River. His parents were slaves, and his father could have been owned by one of several Barnes families listed in Crittenden County.[3] Although many blacks flocked to northern towns to escape from former masters, rural violence, and unpleasant memories, William's folks must not have ventured too far from Crittenden County in the early years of Reconstruction.

Reconstruction was that period immediately following the Civil War when presidential and congressional laws were enacted to reorganize the Confederate states and find solutions to political, economic, and social problems raised by secession and war. In spite of the attempts to ease the transition of blacks into life as freedmen, some states, like Kentucky, made the transition a non-transition.[4]

Freedmen who stayed in Kentucky experienced few of the promises of the Emancipation Proclamation. Kentucky's 1866 legal code contributed significantly to continuation of an atmosphere of intimidation and violence prevalent at the end of the Civil War. Although there were many advances for Kentucky blacks in the three decades after the end of the war, mainly through the efforts of the Freedmen's Bureau, religious organizations, and a growing black leadership, to many the progress had come at terrible physical and spiritual costs.

In *From Slavery to Segregation, 1760–1891*, Marion B. Lucas states, "White society had fought every advancement, and a terrible burden of violence, ignorance, and unrelieved poverty had fallen pitilessly upon the black family."[5]

It is unknown what William's parents did during those Reconstruction years. Perhaps they stayed as freedmen to work for their old master, for most freedmen went to other parts of the same county or to nearby counties, or perhaps they found work as sharecroppers or domestics. Many former masters offered freedmen employment, and some of the older slaves stayed on the masters' lands the rest of their lives.[6]

There may have been other reasons that William's parents stayed in the Crittenden County area. The 1910 census listed William as a mulatto.[7] A mulatto is defined as a person with one black and one white parent. The increase in the number of mulatto slaves was markedly pronounced in the 1850s. Professor Joel Williamson of the University of North Carolina, in a study of miscegenation, wrote, "It was everywhere evident that slavery was getting whiter and whiter, and that planter men themselves bore a significant part of the responsibility for that trend." From the slave's point of view, freedom was less desirable if it meant leaving loved ones behind.[8] This might be true if the loved ones were members of the master's family or even the master himself.

William could read and write and probably was sent to a black school in Crittenden County. After the closing of the Freedmen's Bureau schools, which had been established during Reconstruction, separate, but certainly not equal, public schools had been established for black children in Kentucky. A typical black school might be a leaky old slave cabin heated by a fireplace, where pupils sat on split-log benches and wrote on slates. The school year was short, the program of study limited, and the quality of instruction low, especially in the rural areas.[9] By some statistics, Crittenden and neighboring Livingston County ranked among the best in the rate of black literacy, indicating a better quality of education for black students. In 1900 blacks accounted for 48.2 percent of illiterates in Daviess County, 67.6 percent in Henderson County, and 73.4 percent in McCracken County, just to the north of Crittenden, while only 16 percent of the blacks living in Crittenden and Livingston were illiterate.[10]

Sometime before 1893, William moved down river to the bustling river town of Paducah, where work was more readily available to a young black. Occupational patterns in the river towns were uniform. Blacks worked as common laborers on farms, riverboats, roads, bridges, and railroads. They were also personal servants, garbage collectors, street cleaners, stable hands, maids, waiters, stewards, porters, cooks, nurses, washwomen, barbers, and janitors. They were not hired in factories. In black society the highest rankings were janitors, post office workers, teachers, clergymen, physicians, and attorneys.[11]

In Paducah William met and then married Lemah Jones in 1893, a woman five years his junior.[12] She was born in neighboring Livingston County in 1877, the year Reconstruction ended, and her obituary gives Salem as the town of her birth. One large plantation owner in Livingston County was a William Jones, who died in 1843. Although his dozen slaves were appraised from one hundred to four hundred dollars at his death, there was no sale recorded,[13] indicating that the slaves remained on the Jones place under the ownership of other family members.

During the Civil War many young Livingston County blacks joined the Eighth United States Colored Heavy Artillery Regiment stationed in Paducah,[14] although this was at great risk to their families. The Conscription Act of 1864 ordered the drafting of all able-bodied men between the ages of twenty and forty-five regardless of race, color, condition of servitude, or habitat. Lemah's father probably fell in this category. Many wives and parents were beaten and even killed if their husbands or sons fought for the Union, unless they were released with the blessings of their owners, who would receive three hundred dollars for the loan of the slave.

As with the parents of William Barnes, Lemah Jones's parents seem to have stayed close to the vicinity of their former master's lands. At least they did not cross the Ohio River that bordered their counties and head north to St. Louis or Chicago or Indianapolis or the river towns of Evansville or Mount Vernon. Their children, William and Lemah, would do that.

William and Lemah Barnes stayed in Paducah at least two

years. Their first child, Duke Milton Barnes, was born there sometime in 1895, a child so light that he appeared to be white.[15] By 1897 William, Lemah, and Duke had traveled up the Ohio River, probably by packet boat, to Mount Vernon,

COUNTY HEALTH DEPARTMENT

CERTIFICATE OF BIRTH   MT. VERNON, INDIANA

POSEY COUNTY

THIS IS TO CERTIFY, that our records show:

Name (female) _____ Barns _____ (2nd child born to this mother) _____

Was born in Marrs Township, _____ Indiana, on _____ November 25, __ 19 1897

Child of Wm. Barnes and (X) Jones _____

Birthplace of father Crittenton County, Kentucky Birthplace of mother Livingston County, Kentucky

Record was filed November 25, 1897 ____ Book No. h-4 ____ Page No. 95
                    (Date)

SEAL   John R. Burton M.D.
                                        POSEY COUNTY HEALTH OFFICER

Issued on February 8 __ 19 72

PHONE 838-3196

POSEY COUNTY BOARD OF HEALTH
126 E. THIRD ST. — COLISEUM BLDG.
MT. VERNON, INDIANA 47620

Memo To TO WHOM IT MAY CONCERN ____ Date FEBRUARY 8, 1972

From MRS. HELEN WOLF, CLERK•REGISTRAR
     VITAL RECORDS

I DO HEREBY CERTIFY THE ENCLOSED BIRTH CERTIFICATE IS A TRUE AND CORRECT COPY OF THE
RECORD OF BIRTH, AS RECORDED. CHILD'S NAME (LAST NAME IS SPELLED BARNS) ON THE RECORD
AND THE CHILD'S FATHER'S LAST NAME IS SPELLED BARNES.

                              Mrs. Helen Wolf
                         MRS. HELEN WOLF, CLERK•REGISTRAR
                         POSEY COUNTY BOARD OF HEALTH • VITAL RECORDS

Originals in possession of second daughter-in-law, Alice Louise Martin.

Edna Martin Christian Center Archives

Copy of birth certificate of Edna Mae Barnes. (Original is in possession of Alice Louise Martin, Edna's second daughter-in-law.)

Indiana, where they settled on a farm in Marrs Township. Edna Mae, their second child, was born in Marrs Township on 25 November 1897.[16]

Mount Vernon, Indiana's southern most city, was a shipping point for a rich farming area of approximately one hundred square miles. Thousands of barrels of hominy and flour and tons of hay and corn found their way to the markets of the world from the wharves of Mount Vernon.[17] German and Swiss immigrants had brought in manufacturing and added to the cultural life of the community. Bigham reports that the river continued to be a central focus of residents' lives: "Riverboats, whether floating by or docking in even the smallest places, offered a sense of a larger world outside."[18]

There was quite an active black settlement in Mount Vernon, including schools, although they were inferior to the white schools, and several strong churches. The *Indianapolis Recorder*, "A Negro Newspaper Devoted to the Best Interests of the Colored People of Indiana," frequently printed reports from Mount Vernon and other black communities in the state.[19]

On the day of Edna's birth, the *Mount Vernon Western Star*, whose motto challenged readers to "Dare to Do Right," reported several front-page incidents that reflected the general tempo of the times.

One article described a "Fight on the Levee":

> Last Saturday night the usual fistic [*sic*] carnival occurred on the levee. These engagements are always on the program at the levee for Saturday night and the performance occurs regularly. These gladiatorial contests in which men, women, and children participate, usually occur between the dames and sons of Eth[i]opia, but on this special occasion Christian Eberhart, a white mechanic, was implicated.
>
> Eberhart hails from the northern part of the county, and is employed on the Catholic Church. Saturday evening he went

out in company with others to see the sights. It was not long before his mind was wandering through infinite space toward the stars of the Great Orionic Nebula. The levee was the first and last object of his vision. It was but a few moments until Eberhart was in the thickest of the fray. To use the fistic expression, he was put to "sleep," and did not regain consciousness for some time. Marshal Holloman and his deputy were called, and upon their arrival found Eberhart in an unconscious condition, but after administering stimulants he was revived.[20]

The writer concludes, "The darkies were afterwards arrested and brought to the police court Monday morning, where Henry Gibson plead guilty to the charge of assault and battery, and was fined $20 and sent to jail for 25 days. Willard Johnson and George Doneway plead not guilty, and were sent to jail to await trial."[21]

It was a busy week in Mount Vernon. Another kind of performance besides "fisticuffs" received rave reviews on the same front page. A number of white Mount Vernon ladies provided minstrel entertainment for the citizens of the town by parading through the streets wearing blackface and Mother Hubbards. A few town residents must have had some sensitivities about racial stereotyping, for the article explains, "Whatever may be said for or against the proprietery of ladies minstrels, the introductory one was approved by our people, as was evidenced by the large audience who witnessed it."[22] In scattered society notes on the front page, several people from as far away as Uniontown, Indiana, and Equality, Illinois, came to enjoy the Ladies Minstrel parade, one of the social highlights of the season.

Earlier the newspaper reported that one black man was killed and another seriously injured when run over by the west-bound L & N (Louisville & Nashville) freight train. The two men were identified as Mat Owens and Kelley Hughes, the former from Earlington, and the latter from Marion, Kentucky. For the past three months they worked on a farm opposite Mount Vernon. Hughes explained that he and Owens "were out all night, leaving this city [Mount Vernon] about sun-up on their way to Evansville looking for work." They sat down on the track to rest and fell asleep. The article concluded that the injured Hughes was taken to the poor infirmary and the deceased Owens to the potter's field.[23]

According to the many inches of type in the *Western Star*, Mount Vernon blacks were not faring well the day Edna came into the world, while white citizens were reported visiting friends and family in Evansville, New Harmony, and Cincinnati, celebrating the Ladies' Fair at St. Matthew's Church, attending the Woodmen of the World Lodge social, or enjoying a dance at the elegant Main Street home of the Honorable E. M. Spencer, where Kling's orchestra furnished the music.

Although it would appear that Mount Vernon was not the most hospitable place to raise his young son and baby daughter, William Barnes, by 1900, for some reason moved his growing family across the county line to Evansville, which by the turn of the century had gained the reputation of being the least hospitable of northern gateway cities to blacks.[24] In Evansville the black population had grown from 1,408 in 1870 to 7,405 by 1900, almost 13 percent of the population.[25] Perhaps William was looking for a better job than tilling the rich Posey County river bottom as a sharecropper or hired hand.

In Evansville William was employed as a porter at the Harding & Miller Music Store at 404 Main Street.[26] It is quite significant that he also learned some skills as a piano finisher there. While Evansville enjoyed an upsurge of industrial activity at the turn of the twentieth century, blacks found jobs difficult to obtain. In 1900 less than 4 percent of the black workforce was engaged in manufacturing, and as elsewhere, most were employed at the lowest level—as cleanup workers and porters. Only a handful held skilled positions such as plow grinder, polisher, or machinist.[27] Finisher was certainly a step-up from porter.

Bigham, in his study of Evansville, said that skin pigmentation was an important factor in employment. Those with lighter complexions, who were defined as mulattoes by census takers, as William was, as a rule held jobs with higher status. Higher status jobs for blacks were by custom defined by the degree of contact with and responsibility granted by whites, and at the turn of the century these jobs continued to be associated with those deemed to have mixed blood.[28]

The Barnes family lived at two sites in Evansville, both in Baptisttown,[29] a crowded, undesirable district where housing was dilapidated and furnishings were poor.[30] The quality of black housing was so deplorable that many renters refused to pay rent because of the condition of the homes, but they also refused to vacate because there was nowhere else to live.[31]

When the 1900 census taker arrived at their door on 6 June, William, Lemah, Duke, and Edna lived at 217 Elliott. The census taker wrote Lemah's name as Lamee and checked that both William and Lemah knew how to read and write.[32] A second daughter, Lucille, missed being in the census by three days, born 9 June 1900.[33] The family also lived at 506 East Ohio Street in Baptisttown.

Edna's mother helped make ends meet by doing laundry, cleaning house, or cooking, as she would do for most of her life. These were the usual jobs for uneducated black women and even many of those who were educated. William and the family left Evansville sometime in 1902 before the 1903 Baptisttown riots, although the climate in Evansville was festering toward such a confrontation with increasing racial incidents, loose liquor laws, and overcrowded and demoralizing conditions in Baptisttown.

The Baptisttown riots ignited when Robert Lee, a black man, fatally shot and killed a policeman, Louis Massey, in a gun battle on 3 July 1903 outside a saloon. Mobs threatened to break into the jail and hang Lee, who was critically wounded. Gov. Winfield Durbin called in the local militia to restore order, but just the opposite resulted. A large crowd confronted the one hundred troopers who had surrounded the courthouse. A shot was fired toward the troopers, and the troopers returned fire. Twelve in the crowd were killed and thirty wounded. In return, the governor ordered three hundred militiamen to Evansville, and Lee was moved to the Jeffersonville prison. Lee died before going to trial.

During the weeks of tension, the black community lived in a state of terror as whites decided "to go Negro hunting." One observer noted, "Wherever a Negro was sighted, he was fired upon." Many blacks, afraid for their lives, crowded onto river-boats or fled north by walking along the railroad tracks."[34]

William and Lemah had already reached the capital city of Indiana by the hot, violent Evansville summer of 1903 and were trying to make a new life in the north.

CHAPTER TWO

Scioto Street and a City Built on Sand

At least by 28 December 1902 William and Lemah Barnes lived in Indianapolis because according to Marion County birth records, a fourth child, Thelma, was born to them on that date. Five-year-old Edna Mae was already learning the role of big sister, a role she would never cease playing. The residence of birth was 824 Scioto Street,[1] an alley-like street between stately Meridian Street, with its cedar block pavement, and Pennsylvania Street, lined with arching elms and maples. William and the family lived in two doubles on Scioto Street at various times.

Scioto Street was not in the Fifth and Seventh Wards where most of the blacks lived. Indiana Avenue, the social channel, both legitimate and illegitimate, of the community, linked those two wards together. Along this avenue were "grocery stores, clothing stores, drug stores, three theaters, newspaper offices, barber shops, beauty salons, restaurants, liquor stores, pawnshops, and entertainment spots for the exclusive use by the Black Community."[2]

Indianapolis in 1902 was segregated by custom, not necessarily by law. The 1885 Civil Rights Act prohibited segregation and discrimination in restaurants, hotels, public facilities, and transportation, but it had little legal effect on city practices because of the limited penalty for violation. The act was not amended with stronger penalties for discrimination against blacks until the mid-1940s. Sen. S. Hugh Dillin of Knox and Pike Counties, federal judge of Indiana's southern district, who in the 1980s would become notable as the ruling judge in the desegregation of the Indianapolis Public Schools, enforced the act. Even with the stronger penalties, discrimination of public facilities continued in Indiana cities and towns for many more years.

Indiana historian James H. Madison described the pattern that persisted from the late nineteenth century through the first half of the twentieth century. "Black Hoosiers suffered the burdens of discrimination, segregation, and second-class citizenship in every aspect of their relationship with white Hoosiers. Not only did this sad legacy endure, but there were many areas in which obstacles to black achievement and well-being increased."[3]

The white citizenry, even many educated and so-called liberal thinkers, generally held a deep-seated bias against the migration of blacks, such as the Barnes family, from the South. A 1999 *Indianapolis Star* series on the history of Indianapolis in the last century concluded that political and civic leaders at the beginning of the century "touted Indianapolis as an ideal city made up almost entirely of white, native-born residents. They did not want immigrants or blacks to tarnish that image."[4]

Jacob Piatt Dunn, Jr., civil leader and secretary of the Indiana Historical Society, wrote in his study of Indianapolis in 1910 that in 1900 there were 15,931 blacks inside the city limits, the highest percentage of blacks of any northern city.[5] Hinting caustically about sneaky Republican organization tactics, Dunn, a Democrat, wrote, "It has repeatedly been charged that many negroes were imported here to vote, and there is little reason to doubt it." It was Dunn's opinion that "many objectionable negroes had come to Indianapolis since the southern states began driving out their undesirable classes." He observed, "Most of them have shown a reasonable amount of industry and a smaller number have shown a disposition to save their money and invest it in some permanent form."[6]

Although de facto segregation excluded blacks from parks, theaters, restaurants, hotels, and other public places and from almost all churches, on "the Avenue" and in other pockets of the African-American community blacks created a world of their own. The rising black middle class emulated white society while fostering racial pride and self worth in their own distinctive style. Life was not easy, as there were many restrictions as to where blacks could go and what they could do. That did not mean that life did not have pleasant moments and promises of a more prosperous future.

Every issue of the *Indianapolis Recorder* was filled with social items—who was visiting whom, who was ill, who was entertaining whom, and what was going on at the local clubs.

Miss Ada Booth, of Louisville is the guest of friends in this city.

Robert Williams in Columbia avenue is ill. . . .

Mrs. Anna Mae Davis will entertain her friends at a birthday reception at her home in Bowman street, January 15, from 8 to 11 p.m. . . .

The Up To Date Whist Club was entertained Tuesday evening at the home of Mrs. Mary Johnson in West Fourteenth street.

Mr. and Mrs. Edward Smith will go to Cincinnati Monday for permanent residence. Mr. Smith takes a position on the railroad. . . .

The funeral of Norris Jones occurred last Thursday at the Mt. Zion Baptist Church, under the direction of Shelton and Morgan. . . .

Mr. and Mrs. W. B. Johnson entertained at dinner last Sunday Rev. and Mrs. J. F. Broyles, Rev. and Mrs. L. W. Ratliff[e], Mrs. King and S. A. Ratliffe.[7]

As in any society, there were those who enjoyed the finer

things of life more than others. Not all Indianapolis blacks would have been able to provide a wedding such as that of Sadie Dent and W. A. Lewis, who were married at the home of the bride's mother on North Senate Avenue. The parlors were "tastily decorated with cut flowers and palms. The bride was handsomely gowned in white silk organdy with lace and ribbon trimmings. She wore a veil held in place with orange blossoms and carried a bouquet of bride's roses. . . . Many valuable and handsome presents were received."[8]

In 1902 the *Recorder* published the names of men and women who were worth $5,000 or more. Most were business owners who accumulated their wealth by "hard labor, self denial and small earnings." Many of them had invested their profits in real estate.[9] Funeral home owners were not only successful but also influential in the life of the community. Professionals such as lawyers, physicians, dentists, and teachers were financially stable and also provided valuable leadership. Other successful business ventures included hauling and barbering. Hairstyling, catering, baking, and dressmaking businesses were often owned by women.[10]

Many blacks who moved to Indianapolis, such as the Barnes family, had little education or business enterprise and were barely able to provide food and clothing for their families. After several years working as a laborer around town, William Barnes secured a job as a piano finisher at the Steinway Piano Company, 18 North Pennsylvania Street.[11] Perhaps his earlier experience in the piano factory in Evansville served as an advantage for him. It is difficult to know how long he worked at that location, as, according to family members, he frequently was absent from the home.

"My mother would say he would come home long enough to get a baby and then leave," related Thelma Herrington, one of Edna's sisters, and the Indianapolis city directories seem to substantiate that pattern.[12] Other Indianapolis addresses for the family, beside the 824 Scioto Street address (1902), would

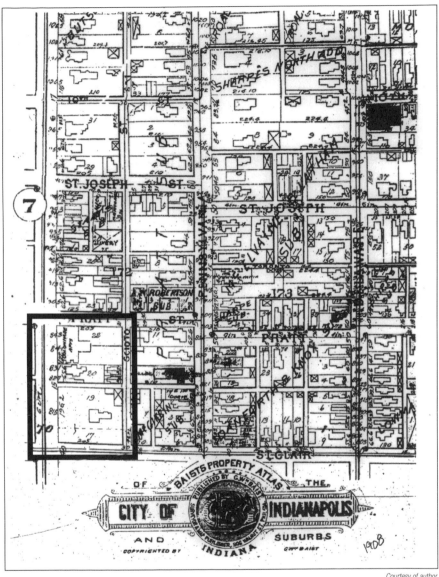

Courtesy of author

1906 map of Scioto Street area showing house sites where the Barnes family lived during its early years in Indianapolis.

include 821 Scioto (1903), 1330 Lafayette (1904), 1221 and 1228 Lafayette (1905, 1906), 435 West Fifteenth, and 321 Cora (1908, 1909). William also did some barbering, and several addresses on the 1300 block of North Senate (1909, 1910) were either home addresses or locations for William's barbershop.[13] In 1912 Lemah was listed as head of the household at the Senate Avenue address.

Duke quit school and went to work as an elevator operator on Pennsylvania Street when he was thirteen. As the oldest son, in the absence of his father, the city directory sometimes listed him as the head of the household. In 1911, 1913, and 1914 he was listed as the head of the household and employed at the American Central Life Insurance Building as an elevator operator. William seems to be with the family at 963 East Georgia in 1915. In 1918 Edna was listed as head of the house at 435 West Fifteenth Street.

According to family members, Duke seemed to have a difficult time finding himself. The fact that he was so light that he could pass for white would be both a bane and a blessing. Leon F. Litwack, author of the Pulitzer prize–winning *Been in the Storm So Long*, wrote in *Trouble in Mind: Black Southerners in the Age of Jim Crow*, "Not only whites placed a premium on shades of color, on class, and on education." Although being a mulatto was generally considered a positive characteristic and may have increased employment opportunities for many, Charles W. Chesnutt, who grew up in North Carolina during Reconstruction, "felt himself to be a virtual exile because of his light complexion." Chesnutt noted in his journal, "I am neither fish[,] flesh, nor fowl. Neither 'nigger,' white, nor 'buckrah.'"[14] Yet others saw a light skin as being a step toward the white standards of beauty. The popularity of skin whiteners and bleaching creams would support this view.

As soon as he or she was old enough, each of the Barnes children worked to supplement their mother's earnings as a cleaning and washwoman. "We were always working and helping my mother, because she washed and we had to pack those clothes back through the forest to the people over on Meridian," Thelma recalled.[15]

Most of the prosperous north side families had hired help. In

Meridian Street north from Fourteenth Street, ca. 1900.

Madison's biography *Eli Lilly: A Life, 1885–1977*, he wrote that Eli and Evelyn Fortune Lilly, who would move to the corner of St. Joseph and Meridian Streets in 1912,[16] usually hired young women from rural Indiana and Kentucky who did the cooking, washing, and ironing.[17] Almost all of the addresses where the Barnes family lived were within half a mile of the Lilly home. Family members tell stories of Edna Mae, a winsome child, struggling to balance a basket of freshly laundered and pressed clothes on her head, striking up back-door associations with the Lillys and other residents of the elite Pennsylvania–Meridian corridor. The 800 block of Scioto Street, where the Barnes family lived after arriving in Indianapolis, was a street of working-class cottages sandwiched between the tree-lined enclaves of regal mansions on Meridian and Pennsylvania Streets. Many of Scioto Street's houses, built in the 1860s,[18] had become decrepit through lack of custodial care.

Many of the elite of Indianapolis society[19] lived in the Meridian and Pennsylvania Street homes, including O. G. Pfaff, Hervey Bates, Jr., Caleb S. Denny, the parents of Booth Tarkington, Postmaster James A. Wildman, Charles D. Meigs, Edward F. Claypool, Charles Mayer, Arthur Jordan, Allen M. Fletcher, J. K. Lilly, and Eli Lilly.

Robert W. Cathcart, who owned the Cathcart and Cleland Bookstore at 26 East Washington Street, lived at 839 North Pennsylvania Street on the southeast corner of Pratt and Pennsylvania Streets, less than a block from 800 Scioto Street. Charlotte "Pink" Cathcart, the Cathcarts' youngest daughter, described neighborhood life in her memoir, from attending card parties to boarding canal boats at Pratt Street for Fairview picnics and from attending May Wright Sewall's Girls' Classical School to donkey-drawn streetcar rides on Pennsylvania Street.[20]

In those gracious Queen Anne and Italianate homes such as the Cathcarts', ladies gathered on pleasant afternoons to sip tea and exclaim over dainty sandwiches made of lemon curd and watercress. In the summer, with their families they attended strawberry socials at Fourth Presbyterian Church, "where tables were set up under the huge walnut trees and the spacious lawn was lit with Japanese lanterns." Cathcart wrote, "This, to a child, was truly fairyland."[21] Cathcart, a self-avowed adventurer and chronicler of the Meridian–Pennsylvania neighborhood from Tinker Street (Sixteenth Street) south to the Circle, never mentions the world on Scioto Street.

Even though Edna and her brother and little sisters could no doubt see the magical Japanese lanterns and the beautiful ladies in their summer dresses from their porch on Scioto Street, their little lane was not a "fairyland." Along with the smell of salt pork frying and corn bread baking was the muted drumming of their mother scrubbing the expensive shirts, lace-trimmed shirtwaists, and delicate linens of the families who lived just a few yards away but in another world.

A street sign announcing Scioto Street still stands just to the north of Meridian Street and midway between the parking lots of the Indianapolis–Marion County Public Library. The library building spans Meridian and Pennsylvania at Eighth Street. Starting in 1901, apartments, flats, and residential hotels began to be built on the 600, 700, and 800 blocks of Pennsylvania Street, and row houses, such as Christian Place at 233 East Ninth Street, began to appear.[22] In 1923 the huge Ambassador apartment building, which is on the National Register of Historic Places, was built back to back to the lots where Edna and her family once lived. The Indianapolis–Marion County Public Library parking lot and a loading dock now nudge over Scioto Street's shabby little lane.

Lessons to Learn

Forced by experience, necessity, and desire, a small but influential middle class, consisting mostly of principals, teachers, housewives, business owners, ministers, church activists, porters, some domestics, and others, took the responsibility for leadership in the black community.[1] They did have help from some white friends. In 1898 Flanner House pioneered social work in the community beginning in a cottage that white funeral home owner Frank Flanner donated for the use of black children. Meager funding limited most programs to self-help efforts featuring lectures and classes by local volunteers. Successful activities included an employment agency that placed female domestics and a day nursery.[2]

A year later the Kings Daughters Society, a group of Indianapolis white women, became worried about children left alone while parents worked. Members rented a room for a nursery at 911 West Washington Street,[3] which would become the Indianapolis Day Nursery Association. In the beginning years, unlike with the Flanner House Program, most of the children served by the organization were white. Support for the program came from an auxiliary formed of white civic leaders and socialites who held charity balls and "silver teas" to raise money.[4]

Although the black society was dominated by males, the major force for positive change came from women. Many educated African-American women, as well as some with little formal education and position, established clubs, organizations, and other agencies. The goals of these black clubwomen were to uplift the race in social, political, and economic areas.[5] Several of these black women served as role models for Edna Barnes Martin in her adolescent years. From them, she learned charity, dignity, self-sufficiency, organizational skills, and much more.

When the Sisters of Charity Hospital was located at Fifteenth and Missouri Streets, the Barnes family lived only two blocks away. Founded in 1874, the Sisters of Charity operated one of the few hospitals in Indianapolis that cared for blacks.[6] Edna would have seen these women dressed in their white-trimmed black outfits as she walked and played in the neighborhood streets. She would have understood that the sisters provided life-and-death services for people such as herself and her family that the white world was not willing to provide.

An apt student, Edna would also learn the spirit of service and the desire to help the less fortunate from excellent black teachers in the Indianapolis Public School (IPS) system, which was segregated although not by law. Since the family moved frequently, she reportedly attended several Indianapolis Public Schools—Numbers 17, 23, and 24.

In 1909, when she was twelve, Edna enrolled at IPS No. 24, and Mary Ellen Cable was her principal. Cable, a leader in the Woman's Improvement Club, had studied at Indiana University, the University of Chicago, and Columbia University. From 1903 to 1905 Cable oversaw the community's elementary school garden project, which ultimately motivated residents in surrounding neighborhoods to plant gardens and improve property. Perhaps Cable's major accomplishment was to organize the Indianapolis branch of the National Association for the

Advancement of Colored People (NAACP) in 1909. As a principal, she emphasized academics and good citizenship.[7]

Not only would Edna have been influenced by Cable, she would also have known about Ada Harris, a teacher and another member of the Woman's Improvement Club, who was making news by "cleaning–up" Norwood on the Indianapolis south side.[8] A newspaper article entitled "Norwood, Once Moral Blot of Marion County, Is Redeemed by Woman" described Harris's impact on the little "colored settlement."[9] By 1909 Harris had taught in Norwood for twenty-one years and had founded a Boys' Club, a Mothers' Club, physical education programs for health and to fight tuberculosis, and self-help programs ranging from shoe repair to cooperatives. Later Harris would say, "My field has been small in Norwood, but it has been plenty large enough for my abilities. At least I shall have spent my life for my race."[10]

Many of the women who were making a difference in the black community were associated with the Indiana State Federation of Colored Women's Clubs, organized by Lillian Thomas Fox, the first African-American reporter for the *Indianapolis News*.[11] In Indiana, as well as in other states, the federation included all-black women's clubs that focused on "religious, moral, educational, or charitable lines."[12] These women had been influenced by W. E. B. Du Bois's concept of the "Talented Tenth," the small, educated minority that would furnish the leadership for uplifting the black masses. Du Bois was the rare black man who was "a supporter of woman suffrage, women's reproductive freedom, and women's economic independence from men."[13]

No doubt a major topic of conversation in the community in 1910 was the announcement that Madam C. J. Walker, the uneducated child of former slaves who was now a millionaire, was moving her hair products and cosmetics company to Indianapolis. That announcement probably gave young black women a sense of pride, as well as excitement, over her glamorous products. However, not everyone was enthralled with

Walker's success. There were those who accused her of trying to make black women in the image of white women with her hair products. Some clergymen even claimed that "if God meant for blacks to have straight hair, he would have endowed them with it."[14]

Madam Walker's contributions to the welfare of the black community, as much as her business successes, were well known.[15] Black women earned less than any other working group in America. In the first decade of the twentieth century, few black women earned more than $1.50 per week. During this same period, the average unskilled white worker earned about $11 weekly. By 1912 Walker had trained more than one thousand women as beauty culturists, many of them making $10 to $15 a day. "I have made it possible for many colored women to abandon the wash-tub for more pleasant and profitable occupation,"[16] Madam Walker claimed.

Sometime during the years from 1911 to 1914, Edna attended Shortridge High School, which was then located on

Shortridge High School, ca. 1905.

Pennsylvania between North and Michigan Streets. The high school occupied three buildings. The oldest was two stories high with a large study hall on the second floor. The Annex was a classroom building that contained the art studios. The newest building, built in 1904, was a three-story structure with the main entrance on North Street. In the center was an auditorium, Caleb Mills Hall, and on the lower level was the gymnasium. Around this core were classrooms and science laboratories.

The few blacks that attended high school at that time in Indianapolis were enrolled at Shortridge, Arsenal Technical, and Emmerich Manual Training high schools. However, they were not given the chance to be active members of the student body. All sports and clubs were segregated, and frequently there was enforced segregated seating in the classrooms and cafeterias.[17]

Shortridge had exceptional teachers, many with advanced degrees from prestigious schools such as Columbia, Cornell, and the University of Chicago. One of the teachers was Laura Donnan, with undergraduate and graduate degrees from the University of Michigan. Renowned for her course in American government, she was also known for demanding that her students memorize large portions of the Bill of Rights. She was a strong advocate for "the rights of blacks."[18]

In addition to the imposed racial restrictions, high school was not easy for Edna. First, she had to walk five miles a day to and from school, and then she had no money for lunch. The smell of food coming from the cafeteria was often more than she could bear.[19] Family members attest that Edna finished the high school course, although no record of her graduation has been located.

By Edna's seventeenth birthday, there were seven children in the family—Duke, Edna, Lucille, Thelma, Marie, Harold, and Arletta. Lemah struggled to find ways to maintain the home, and the children drew close together to support their mother. Lemah had to have been strong to keep her brood in school, off the streets, and out of trouble.

The entry of the United States into World War I on 6 April 1917, along with the resulting shortage of male workers, opened jobs to black women that normally would not be available. But opportunities for black men and women were normally limited to the least desirable work.[20]

All through her youth Edna worked long hours outside the home. Among other jobs, she worked as a housemaid, at a clay factory on Fourteenth and Missouri Streets, as a waitress in 1918, and as a clerk in 1920 at Allison Coupon Company. Once, a sister recalled, "They had to carry Edna home when she collapsed from fatigue and hunger downtown."[21] The doctor diagnosed tuberculosis, and after a period of convalescence, she recovered completely.[22]

From the experiences of her youth, Edna learned to identify with her mother and the women in her community who were poverty-stricken, poorly paid, and sorely treated. She knew that women could make a difference. Women could be strong. In fact, women had to be strong to take care of themselves, as well as to take care of those who could or would not take care of themselves.

Edna's Church, Her Cornerstone

What really molded and fired Edna Martin's personality besides the impressions left by her mother, her teachers, and other community role models, was the influence of her church, Mount Zion Missionary Baptist Church. When she began attending the church, it was a brick building, built in the early 1900s, located at Twelfth and Fayette Streets. In 1960 the congregation relocated to an imposing Gothic stone facility at Thirty-fifth Street and Graceland Avenue. A member of the Progressive National Baptist Convention, a black church organization, and the American Baptist Convention, a white church organization, Mount Zion was affiliated with the Indianapolis Baptist Association, which would later support the East Side Christian Center.

Most historians agree that the church was and is the most influential institution in the black community, although its power base saw a shift in the last quarter of the twentieth century, especially after the assassination of Dr. Martin Luther King, Jr., and the move away from King's message of nonviolence and Christian love.

During slavery and at least up to the mid–twentieth century, religious faith and church affiliation enabled blacks to survive and endure. The church—the center for social, educational, and charitable activities—helped develop leaders, both men and women. Barred from other fields of activity open to men, black women found that "the church offered opportunities for self-fulfillment and service" that they could receive nowhere else.[1] Although prohibited according to tradition and interpretations of religious doctrine from official positions of church leadership, black women possessed enormous resources of time and commitment. Ministers who were not blinded by a bias against women in leadership positions found that women could provide a rich resource of time and talent. However, there was still a clear line as to what women could and could not do in the church community.

Black churches could not have survived without the active support of black women. In spite of their importance in the life of the church, serving as missionaries, deaconesses, lay readers, Sunday school teachers, musicians, counselors, and secretaries, the offices of preacher and pastor in the historic black churches remained a male preserve and were not generally available to women.[2] In her book, *When the Truth Is Told: A History of Black Women's Culture and Community in Indiana, 1875–1950*, Darlene Clark Hine writes that "black women propelled the church towards service as a welfare agency and shaped it into an institution for social as well as spiritual uplift. They realized the urgent necessity of connecting the church more closely with the things of the world in order to make that world a decent place in which to live. For them, the building of a Christian character meant that the church and its members had to exert more influence on or control over the social forces which threatened the stability of their homes, family, and communities."[3]

By available accounts, organized religion did not play much of a role in Edna's life until her teenage years. Edna was seventeen when Rev. George W. Ward, pastor at Mount Zion, baptized her. At her church she would learn the tenets of the Christian faith—obedience to the Gospel and love of the Bible, plus the tools of her future trade—missionary teacher and children's worker. At her church she would also learn to seek middle-class values and lifestyles.

One of her first missionary deeds was to bring her mother and her brothers and sisters into the church, where they also were baptized.[4] Her evangelistic work did not stop there. At nineteen, she became vice president of the Lott Carey Missionary Society, named for a black preacher who went to Africa in the 1820s under the auspices of Baptists in America and the American Colonization Society. During those years Edna dreamed of becoming a missionary to Africa. One of her proudest accomplishments in the Lott Carey Missionary Society was to help raise funds for a hospital in Liberia. She continued her leadership of the society until after her marriage

Indiana Historical Society

Senate Avenue YMCA.

to Earl Martin on 12 September 1921.

Mount Zion was the approved dating agency for the young members. "Momma always kept us interested in the church and Sunday school. We would get ready and go and then we would go right back in the afternoon to BYPU [Baptist Young People's Union]; we met our boyfriends [there],"[5] Edna's sister Thelma Herrington recalled.

In Edna's case, it was not at church that she met her husband-to-be, although he was a member of Mount Zion. According to a later account,[6] the two met at a Senate Avenue YMCA Monster Meeting, where large numbers (hence the name) gathered for public forums. National and local African-American leaders discussed racial themes and issues at these assemblies. Evangelistic in nature, the Monster Meeting was one of the largest gatherings of men in the country. Many of the events and meetings were also open to women. In 1916, under the leadership of Senate Avenue YMCA Executive Secretary Faburn E. DeFrantz, the event became even more progressive and influential in the molding and shaping of the opinions and beliefs of the black community.[7]

Earl's mother's family, the Valentines, were charter members of the Senate Avenue YMCA,[8] as well as charter members of Mount Zion when it was organized in Fletcher's Bottom on the Indianapolis south side in 1869. Raised in the church, Earl understood the role of churchwomen in the community, and he was always supportive of Edna's efforts. Edna taught Sunday school and organized the Willing Workers Club, dedicated to performing acts of charity for the needy of the community. She became an active member of the National Sunday School Association, the National Baptist State Women's Convention, and eventually Church Women United, along with many other similar groups. Through the encouragement of her church, Edna took course work in the Church Federation's "Winning the Children for Christ" program, and she received a diploma, one of the first black women to achieve that recognition in Indianapolis.

Mount Zion did more than offer Sunday worship and Bible studies. It provided multiservices for members and the community from birth to death—inspiring, teaching, helping, organizing, and leading. An article describing the history of the church written in 1970 explains, "The total influence for good exerted by Mt. Zion in the Indianapolis community cannot be measured. Thousands of souls have been taught God's Word, have received solace and comfort in times of distress and sorrow and have gone forth to help others."[9]

In the early days of her marriage, not even pregnancy would deter Edna from her daily church activities. "We used to laugh," a sister joked, "when Edna was expecting their first child, and say, 'Edna was going to drop that baby going to the missionary [society] and coming back up and down the canal.'"[10] Edna loved her church, and she soaked up its teachings at all levels. She would remain active in Mount Zion until her death, and her funeral would be conducted in the sanctuary she loved among her friends of almost a lifetime.

Life in the City and a Song Gone

Not only did the church play an important role in Edna and Earl Martin's marriage, the couple immersed themselves in community organizations such as the Senate Avenue YMCA, where Earl was a member of executive secretary R. K. Smith's Men's Fellowship, a group that included many prominent leaders in the community. Earl also played in the YMCA band. Edna also loved music. She had taken classes at the Indiana College of Music (later Jordan School of Music), played the piano, and sang soprano at many church events. Earl was a graduate of the Cosmopolitan School of Music, founded in 1919 by Lillian LeMon, a charter member and early president of the Indiana Music Promoters, a branch of the National Association of Negro Musicians. The Cosmopolitan School of Music was more than just a place to study music. Both students and teachers played an active role in helping to determine the destiny of the black community.[1]

When Earl secured a job as a postal carrier,[2] the Martins entered the ever-growing black middle class. In the early years of their marriage they lived at two different addresses on

Fayette Street near Mount Zion Missionary Baptist Church. In August 1922 Edna and Earl became parents to a baby girl, Doris Lillian, likely named after good friend and music mentor Lillian LeMon. Two years later a son and namesake, Earl William Martin, Jr., completed the family. Many middle-class blacks such as the Martins were purchasing homes on the city's north side. Such a decision by the Martin family brought them face-to-face with new realities about life in Indianapolis.

The black population of Indianapolis was increasing dramatically in the 1920s. The *Indianapolis Star* reported that "a migration of blacks north after World War I increased the black population in Indianapolis from 34,678 in 1920 to 43,967 in 1930."[3] However, the situation for members of the black community worsened significantly in the 1920s with the rise of the Ku Klux Klan. The Klan dominated the city hall, the school board, and the police department. It was a reign of terror with acts of vandalism, crosses burned, anonymous letters, warning telephone calls, and "threats chalked on doorways and sidewalks."[4] The Klan was not a fringe group, Emma Lou Thornbrough points out in her study of blacks in Indiana. "Klan members came from every stratum of society—farmers, factory workers, businessmen, professionals, and ministers. . . . It is estimated that at least 25 percent of all native-born white males in the state were Klan members."[5]

"We had, in effect, apartheid here in Indianapolis," Alan T. Nolan, a former attorney for the local chapter of the National Association for the Advancement of Colored People, said in a series in the *Indianapolis Star*. "This town was bitterly divided. The schools were rigidly segregated. The housing was rigidly segregated. A black person couldn't sit downstairs in a movie theater. There was a black YMCA and a white YMCA."[6]

As blacks moved farther north in Indianapolis, anxious whites formed the White Citizens Protective League. A headline in the 26 July 1924 issue of the *Indianapolis Freeman*, a local black paper, read, "White Supremacy Leaguers Plan War on North End." The article notified its readers that some whites in the area planned a rally protesting against black families moving to the north side. A handbill announcing the protest meeting encouraged the presence of white residents saying, "If you are a red-blooded-white American, do not let any trivial excuse keep you away. Your next door neighbor may soon be a nigger."[7]

White property owners resorted to a number of peaceful yet unconstitutional methods to keep blacks out of their neighborhoods. They formed civic leagues that were instrumental in passing a 1926 zoning ordinance that "made it illegal for a person to move into a neighborhood where current residents were primarily of a different race without the consent of a majority of the residents of the opposite race."[8] The ordinance further stated that it was "advisable to foster the separation of the white and Negro residential communities."[9]

Blacks were denied home mortgages by banks and kept out of neighborhoods by restrictive covenants. "When these methods failed, whites resorted to harassment or violence to intimidate black home buyers in all-white neighborhoods."[10] One of the more violent attacks occurred in the early summer of 1924. A hand grenade shattered the windows of the John B. Johnson home at 601 West Twenty-eighth Street. While the percussion of the grenade tossed them out of bed, no one was hurt. Two white men were arrested for the crime shortly afterward. Not deterred, blacks continued moving into the area. It was a matter of pride and knowledge of their rights and privileges as citizens.

W. E. B. Du Bois, author of the classic *The Souls of Black Folk, Essays and Sketches*, which influenced many in the black community in the twentieth century, and originator of "The Talented Tenth" concept, spoke at a rally in Indianapolis in 1925. In his speech he emphasized that blacks wanted "to make it possible for a man to be both a Negro and an American without being cursed and spit upon by his fellows, without having the doors of Opportunity closed roughly in his face."[11]

Judge Henry J. Richardson, Jr., who was the first black

elected to the Indiana General Assembly (1932), described the situation in Indianapolis in 1925: "Most [blacks] lived on the westside and a very few on the eastside and none on the north-side north of 25th Street, as the law prohibited them from living north of 30th Street." He explained, "Any minority citizen who went beyond 30th Street, even the servants, had to have iden-tifications or they were hauled in by the Klan police power."[12] Few blacks lived on the south side, which was peopled mainly by white residents formerly from Kentucky and Tennessee.

In 1929 the Martins moved their family north, first to the 2700 block and then to a house on the 2500 block of Indianapolis Avenue, a few blocks from the scene of the 1924 violence against the Jackson family on West Twenty-eighth Street. Twelve years later, when Harry Lee Pettrie, a Crispus Attucks High School teacher for many years, and his school-teacher wife purchased a house at Twenty-fifth Street and Indianapolis Avenue, they paid $2,000 for the home with a down payment of $50. In an *Indianapolis Star* article, Abe Aamidor stated, "They had to buy the house 'on contract,' meaning the seller financed the deal, because no bank would give them a mortgage."[13]

Late in the decade the depression created even more problems for Indianapolis blacks with mass unemployment and increased poverty. Earl Martin was fortunate to have a secure job with the postal service, unlike the two thousand black laborers (foundry men, porters, janitors, elevator operators, and domestic servants) who by the end of 1929 had lost their jobs as whites replaced blacks.[14] Edna was also fortunate; she did not have to work outside the home.

Edna enjoyed her family life and especially delighted in her children. Doris Lillian shared her parents' musical talents, inheriting her mother's singing talent. Doris had a beautiful voice and sang in the Mount Zion junior choir. An article in the *Indianapolis Recorder* reported that she appeared in a church musical along with her aunts, Thelma and Lucille.[15]

Doris Lillian Martin and Earl Martin, Jr., children of Edna and Earl Martin. Doris Lillian died suddenly at the age of fourteen, apparently due to appendicitis.

The children attended the school in the area, Indianapolis Public School No. 42. In 1936 Doris Lillian, an excellent scholar, was a student at the segregated Booker T. Washington Junior High School. She was looking forward to entering Crispus Attucks High School, which was an all-black high school that opened in 1927. Considerable controversy had surrounded the school's creation. Although local Klan supporters urged the building of Attucks, the project also had the backing of such mainstream groups as the Indianapolis Chamber of Commerce and the Federation of Community Civic Clubs. The "local chapter of the NAACP sought unsuccessfully to block the school's construction on the grounds that students would not receive an equal education in a separate school."[16]

Fears that Attucks would provide an inferior level of education were quickly proved unjustified. It became an excellent school with a faculty that boasted many graduate and doctoral degrees. For many years Attucks had a higher graduation rate than the city's white schools.[17] Edna and Earl were looking forward to their precocious daughter starting her high school years.

On 18 January 1937 the telephone rang, and Edna rushed to the school to take a sick fourteen-year-old Doris Lillian to St. Vincent Hospital. Less than a week later Doris Lillian was dead. Appendicitis was the cause of death, as noted in the newspaper death notice.[18] "It like to have killed Edna," her sister Thelma remembered. "It like to have killed all of us."[19]

Her heart broken, her faith shaken, Edna listlessly walked through the daily routines of her church work and cared for her husband and son. She would not touch her piano. She would not sing a note. For now, her song was gone.

CHAPTER SIX

Rejuvenation and Revival

E dna Martin's mother, Lemah Barnes, who raised her
family without much help from her husband by doing
wealthy people's laundry, passed away on 4 April 1940.[1]
Edna and Earl had done what they could over the years to
make life more comfortable for Lemah. As a teenager Edna
had brought her mother into Mount Zion Missionary
Baptist Church and encouraged her to be active. Spring
1940 found Edna contemplating her mother's death, her
daughter's death, and perhaps her own mortality.

It was big news for the whole Indianapolis church commu-
nity when the *Indianapolis Recorder* reported on 20 April
1940 that "30,000 Baptists Await Training Conference at Mt.
Zion April 22–6." Edna's church, Mount Zion, was one of the
ninety-three white and black churches that were part of the All
Baptist Fellowship, organized in 1939 to promote racial, reli-
gious, and cultural exchanges. The brainchild of Rev. J. T.
Highbaugh, pastor of Good Samaritan Baptist Church, the All
Baptist Fellowship represented the Union District of the
National Baptist Convention, the Central District of the
National Baptist Convention, and the Indianapolis Baptist

Association of the Northern Baptist Convention (now American Baptist Churches USA).[2]

Unlike the Interracial Committee of the Church Federation, which was formed in 1921 with a traditional composition of one black and four whites, the members of the All Baptist Fellowship desired to enter into a more balanced and personal dialogue with one another. There were seventeen thousand black Baptists and thirty thousand white Baptists involved in the alliance.

The speakers for the rally all had national reputations, including Dr. John W. Thomas, director of the American Baptist Home Mission Society; Dr. H. M. Smith, dean of the Chicago Baptist Training Institute; and local leaders Rev. John Hall of Second Baptist Church, Rev. C. H. Bell of Mount Paran Baptist Church, and Rev. S. W. Hartsock, chairman of the Interracial Committee of Indianapolis Baptist Association. Over the five-day session, Edna and other attendees learned skills in witnessing, organization of programs, and in the creation of a "common Baptist front, across racial and organizational lines."[3]

In Hebrew, the name "Edna" means rejuvenation. By her own account, Edna Martin's moment of rejuvenation began on her twentieth wedding anniversary, Sunday, 12 September 1941. Through prayer and meditation, she had been beseeching God to remove the bitter despair over her daughter's death. She had attended the Church Federation's National Christian Teaching Mission in November 1940, and the evangelistic fervor of the international and national Christian leaders who spoke at the meetings touched her heart.[4] Edna told a friend, "God spoke to me." Referring to her deceased daughter Doris Lillian, she said, "I loved her so much, too much. I put her before everything and everyone, even God. God took her to teach me that no one comes before Him and His will."[5] Edna answered God's "call" by traveling across town to the Martindale community.

By the 1940s Indianapolis had a reputation as one of the worst offenders against civil rights among American cities. African-

American workers encountered flagrant discrimination in employment opportunities and union memberships, and most public facilities were still segregated. Although the Indianapolis branch of the National Association for the Advancement of Colored People (NAACP) successfully challenged the constitutionality of the 1926 zoning ordinance, segregation in the city's housing, restaurants, parks, employment, theaters, hospitals, and public schools remained in force.

Migrants from other towns and states were flooding into the capital city looking for wartime jobs. Even if blacks could find jobs, they could not find adequate housing. A Citizens Housing Committee report released in 1940 described slum areas where most of the black population lived and said that "unregulated building of low cost frame structures without sanitary facilities, was for many years, allowed to take place. Such areas were bad to start with, and grew worse as they grew older."[6] The Martindale area was one of these blighted areas.

Yearning for a better life, blacks journeyed to Indianapolis from the southern states in the post–Civil War period to build homes and churches. Instead of moving into Ward Five or Ward Seven around Indiana Avenue, where most blacks lived, the newcomers congregated to the northeast of downtown, in an area known as Martindale.

Between 1916 and 1920 approximately half a million black southerners headed to the industrial cities of the North, including Indianapolis, and a million more would follow in the 1920s.[7] Many came to the Martindale area to reunite with family members, hoping jobs, although probably only menial, might be available at the Indianapolis Car Works Brightwood yard[8] or in other area industries.[9] From the founding of the Martindale community to the years after World War I, the reign of the Ku Klux Klan, the Great Depression, and a slowdown at the Brightwood railroad yards, the houses once built with bright hopes became ramshackle and rodent ridden. Generations of discouragement, dissipation, and disenfranchisement corrupted lives and ideals and left the littered streets ruled by violence and crime, much of it inflicted by youths.

Along with the problems of social and economic discrimination came the escalation of violence and crime in the black community. In 1941 a survey by the city of Indianapolis found that 75 percent of its crime was committed on the near eastside. The Indianapolis Church Federation, supported by research, identified a high rate of juvenile delinquency in the same area.

Edna took the Church Federation's report on conditions in the Martindale neighborhood as a personal challenge. Someone had to do something to help the children described in the report. For Edna Mae Barnes Martin, it was a "Here am I, Lord, send me" epiphany. She had no advanced degrees and no financial or political clout. She was not a trained social worker, but she had been prepared well at Mount Zion to minister to children.

It was not unusual for black women to start day care centers or free kindergartens. In 1909 when Edna was twelve, four women started a free kindergarten at 426 West Twelfth Street, not far from her home. The *Recorder* reported, "The rooms of the building have been made very attractive with new paper and paint. Everything presents a very pleasing and comfortable appearance. The enrollment of over 60 children has greatly encouraged the promoters. The parents are being asked to contribute [a] small sum of ten cents per week to defray the expenses. Mrs. Lillian Brown desires to thank the friends, churches, the Woman's Club and the Woman's Improvement Club for donations given her, thereby making it possible to open the school."[10]

What was unusual was that Edna had ventured out on her own, without support from friends or donations from churches or clubs. Though she had little seed money, just what she could squeeze from her household budget, and although she did not live in the targeted area, Edna set out to rescue the children at risk in the Martindale area, also called Oak Hill. Fired up by her experiences in the All Baptist Fellowship, Mount Zion's association with the Church Federation, and the "Winning the Children for Christ" program, she was convinced that God "had called her out" to rescue the children in that neighborhood.

In fall 1941, without financial or institutional support, she rented a room for fourteen dollars a month in the apartments on Norman Court, 1475 Roosevelt Avenue,[11] an area now intersected by Interstate 70. Edna knew that black women had opened day nurseries in other parts of the city and in Evansville for the children of working mothers and that sometimes these facilities were funded from contributions from blacks as well as from whites.[12] She wanted her day nursery to be different. Instead of offering just babysitting, social skills, and recreational opportunities,[13] Edna wanted to win the children for Christ.

She rode the streetcar, toting pails and rags from home, and took soap and water to the rented room's grimy floors. She borrowed chairs and a few tables and was soon ready for the task at hand. On her first day in business two little sisters appeared on the doorstep of the apartment house.

With her starter duo, Edna went door to door and gathered other children of working mothers until the little space on Norman Court was overflowing. Her funds for the meager rent ran out within a year, and Edna was forced to find a new location for her ministry. The start of World War II and its rationing added to the difficulty. However, Edna prevailed, relocating in an unused circus tent.[14] After her retirement, Edna described this tent experience to Virginia Sutton:

> When we were told that we would have to move from the building, because of being behind with our rent, a friend came to our rescue and rented a large tent. How thrilled we were with that tent! We had services in there and actually had real circuses where the children drew lifesize lions, tigers and bears.

We had become like a real family now and no one wanted to go home. Everyone wanted to stay. We had to depend on the Lord for our needs to be taken care of, and always they were met. As I recall, our largest contribution at that time was $5.

One day the driver of a bakery truck stopped and asked if we could use some day-old bakery products. This was like manna from heaven. It was wonderful. The bakery man became interested and would bring us candy.

The large boys, many of them six feet tall, would stay outside and play basketball. I wondered how I would ever handle and reach this large number of big boys who kept coming. Then one day I called them together on the playground and said, "You know this is a Christian Center and I am a missionary. Somehow we have got to pause a moment and thank God for the blessings of the day. I wonder how many of you would be willing to do that?" Every hand went up. These were grown boys.

Each day at four o'clock I rang the bell. Every boy stopped his jumping at once and bowed his head and we had prayer together. We named it "the pause that refreshes."

We charged the kindergarten children ten cents a day. If they didn't have ten cents we ate together anyway. I'll never know where we got the food, but every day we had something.

I bought a tin tub and gave baths, scrubbed heads, and sent the children home clean.[15]

Once she made her mind up, she never looked back. She believed in the edict of Ecclesiastes 5:4, "When you vow to God, do not delay paying it; for he has no pleasure in fools." She would find and create a clean, safe space for the children of the blighted area of Martindale.

CHAPTER SEVEN

The Winds Shall Not Prevail

Edna Martin's work did not go unnoticed. In the fall of 1945 she was interviewed by an All Baptist Fellowship committee consisting of Mary Trent, wife of the pastor of Woodruff Place Baptist Church, a white church on the near east side; Rev. J. T. Highbaugh, pastor of Good Samaritan Baptist Church in the black community; and Clive McGuire, pastor of Garden Baptist Church, a white church located on Bright Street in Edna's childhood neighborhood. Satisfied with her motivations and abilities, the All Baptist Fellowship began sponsoring her efforts, and the East Side Christian Center was born.

White Baptist churches in the All Baptist Fellowship had experience operating a Christian center. The American Baptist Home Mission Society established its first Christian center in Hammond, Indiana, following World War I. Brooks House was created to serve European immigrants who had come to work in the steel mills.[1] Since the fall of 1943, the All Baptist Fellowship had been active in the Indianapolis black community, sponsoring the West Side Christian Center under the direction of Mattie D. Grigsby Anderson, who had come from an American Baptist Christian center in Detroit to establish a program. The next year, Anna Bybee, a member of Good Samaritan Baptist Church, became director of the West Side Christian Center. The purpose of both East Side and West Side Centers was to reach children in and out of church with the message of Christ and with an incentive to live a Christian life.

Reverend Highbaugh frequently declared that Edna Martin was one of the pioneers in the children's work field. Edna's work would outlive the west side mission. Her pastor at Mount Zion Missionary Baptist Church, Rev. R. T. Andrews, perhaps provided the reason for Edna's success: "Edna could detect a child in need twenty miles away."[2]

Frequently Edna would recite a poem that reflected her philosophy about why children were so important to her:

> In hearts too young for envy,
> There lies the way to make men free.
> Let child love child, and strife will cease
> Disarm the heart, for that is peace.[3]

The Newsette, *August-September, 1947*

Children in playground of East Side Christian Center on Martindale Avenue, 1947. Edna Martin is in the background.

The Newsette, *August-September, 1947*

Children's choir, East Side Christian Center, Martindale Avenue, 1947, standing in front of New Bethel Missionary Baptist Church. The children loved singing, and their voices brought more children into the already crowded Center.

Now with help from the All Baptist Fellowship, Edna moved her mission into a three-room shotgun house at 1519 Martindale, present-day Dr. Andrew Brown Avenue. The house was one of the original structures of the New Bethel Missionary Baptist Church, and it adjoined the church.[4] Although the house had no water or toilet facilities, children soon packed the rooms. Edna recalled in later years that "the church next door had no vision of what we were trying to do at the time and did not allow us to go in, even to use the toilet."[5] Edna had no choice but to use the street hydrant or pay the church twenty-five cents per bucket of water. In the winter the sole source of heat was a potbellied stove that often smoked out the inhabitants of the building. It was so cold in the house that she would work the entire day without removing her boots, coat, or gloves. "These were hard times and the Lord only knows how we were able to stay with it," Edna remembered.

Across the street from the Martindale location of the East Side Christian Center and New Bethel Missionary Baptist

Church was John Hope (Indianapolis Public School No. 26). The Center soon became a magnet, attracting children as they poured from the building at the end of classes. "The children were loud, boisterous and unclean. You have never seen anything like the way they were. Their clothes were tattered and they were hungry. They stayed out of school when they wanted to, played cards on the church steps, and nobody cared,"[6] Edna recalled in 1974. Edna's first project was a children's choir, and the kids loved to sing the gospel choruses. Out on the street, other boys and girls would hear the bright, peppy songs, and Edna became a Pied Piper as children followed her into the shabby little wooden structure. Soon, so many were there that there was no room left.

However, among the mass of little bodies in the crowded room, things began to disappear— supplies and personal items, including Edna's gold watch. One day after taking a quick inventory, and almost despairing of the situation, she wearily drew the cluster of noisy little ones around her. She began quietly to tell them Bible stories of Jesus's parables and God's love. Soon they were still, their bodies no longer fidgeting, their faces tilted up to her gentle gaze and the sound of her voice.

> Or what woman, if she has ten silver coins and loses one coin, does not light a lamp and sweep the house and search carefully until she finds it?
>
> And when she has found it, she calls together her friends and neighbors, saying, "Rejoice with me, for I have found the coin which I had lost!"
>
> In the same way, I tell you, there is joy in the presence of the angels of God over one sinner who repents.[7]

As her words began to sink in, one by one little boys and girls, eyes downcast, came up to her and handed her things they had taken—crayons, scissors, books, and her watch. Edna believed that "Jesus had touched their hearts and they were repentant."[8]

Although the Center was constantly in financial trouble, Edna saw that the children always had something to eat. "She would go to a local supermarket to buy the cheapest items: chicken wings at ten cents a pound and turnip greens at seven cents a can. Edna and her work were well known, and as she walked down the aisles people usually gave her enough money to pay for the food in her basket. The manager of the Allison's Division of General Motors factory cafeteria in Indianapolis would save all the chicken backs for the Center. Edna would then gather a troupe of women who would pick the meat off the bones and make casseroles, which were frozen and later served to the children."[9]

Edna ventured into places most churchwomen would not go. The Nineteenth Hole Saloon at Nineteenth and Martindale, called by locals the "Bucket of Blood" because of all the fights,[10] was certainly not a proper place for Edna, but she was not intimidated by the setting. Edna would enter the bar with her hair neatly combed back from her normally friendly, light brown face, her back straight in her prim flowered dress, and she would stride unsmiling across the smoke-filled room. The men standing along the bar and sitting around bottle-cluttered tables would draw back and try to fade into the grimy walls. They knew what she wanted—fathers who were spending their families' grocery money on booze. She knew many were there because they were out of work and discouraged, but she wanted them out of the Bucket of Blood and the other taverns in the neighborhood. She would not leave until she had shamed them out the door and on their way home, hopefully with money left in their pockets for groceries and rent.[11]

Edna knew what alcohol could do. Her father frequently deserted the family because of drink, and her older brother Duke was a victim of alcohol, landing on Edna's doorstep many times unable to take care of himself. She saw mothers and children every day who were suffering because of fathers drowning in alcohol addiction. She would put her life on the line to keep that from happening to other families.

Although the Martindale site was larger than the original location, Edna soon discovered she was overrun, not only by children but also by rats and bugs. With a broom always within reach to fend off the unwelcome pests, Edna undauntedly gathered her family and friends to staff the Center. Marjorie Bell, a coworker with Edna in the Woman's Baptist Convention of the National Baptist Convention, was one of the first workers at the Center. Betty Mae Watts Kuhn and Blanche Squires were also early assistants in the work. Edna's sister, Thelma Herrington, and her niece, Deloris Mitchell, joined her later. Rebecca Woods served as the Center's first cook.

Life on Martindale was not easy. Not only were there problems with rodents and roaches, but city health inspectors would also order the children off the premises because of the unsafe

The Newsette, *August-September, 1947*

The three-room shotgun house at 1519 Martindale Avenue was soon overrun with children. After school, children of all ages would flock to the Center for prayers, music, food, Bible stories, and crafts.

and unhealthy conditions. "We would comply," Edna recalled later, "but the little ones would stand outside against the building. It was cold at home. We would bring them back in."[12]

To empower the children with a sense of self-worth, Edna designed programs and activities that taught them moral and spiritual lessons, using familiar cultural traditions to facilitate learning. *The Newsette*, the Baptist Youth Fellowship newspaper, described a typical class this way: "The primaries have charge of the opening period of worship. . . . One of the girls reads a Psalm as a call to worship. They sing a familiar hymn and then all heads are bowed while the boys and girls thank God in short prayers for their food, clothing, families, churches, and the beauties of the world."[13] The "call to worship" on this day involved a reading of scripture from the Gospel of Matthew and a response. Using the approach of active participation rather than passive listening, teachers and pupils had a shared experience from the start.

A former student, Jo Diane Westmoreland Ivey, was enrolled in the Center as a two year old, and she grew up there. "I never will forget Mrs. Herrington [Edna's sister] teaching us 'Jesus Wants Me for a Sunbeam.'" Ivey also remembered the Bible-based plays the children were involved in, such as "Cleopas and his friend," the story of two men who met Jesus on the road to Emmaus. The men did not recognize Jesus, who had risen from the tomb, and upon his inquiries, they shared with Him their grief at his crucifixion and reports of His resurrection. Jesus revealed himself to them and they went away rejoicing.[14] "We all learned to be hams, but the plays built confidence, pride, and self-expression in the children," Ivey recalled.[15] Mrs. Martin "planted those kinds of seeds in my head early" to be a missionary, Ivey said. Although Ivey did not become a missionary in the sense that Edna may have had in mind, she did join the Peace Corps and worked with VISTA (Volunteers in Service to America).[16]

A biblical play frequently used in the boys' programs was "Joseph and His Brothers." The plot described how Joseph's brothers, overcome with jealousy, sold him into slavery. The brothers told their father that Joseph was killed, causing him to wail in grief upon hearing of his most-loved son's death. Because of his ability to interpret dreams, Joseph rose to a position of power in Egypt. When he had the opportunity to get revenge on his brothers during a famine, he instead showed mercy and brought about reconciliation of the family.[17]

Edna would gather the exuberant little boys, draped in the makeshift robes of the jealous brothers, and the one chosen to be Joseph, clothed in a patchwork many-colored coat, around her. "Now children, listen to me. That was a mean thing for those brothers to do to their little brother, wasn't it?" Little heads would nod in vigorous agreement. "But that brother who was sold as a slave still had God's favor. He did not hate his brothers. He remembered how much his father had loved him. And because he listened to God, he rose above slavery to be an important man in a land not his own."

Rev. Joshua Cutler, one of those little boys who became a pastor in several Indiana and Kentucky cities, remembered Edna clearly. She was "a little lady, very gentle, kind, walking myself and many other kids to the East Side Christian Center during the week." Cutler, a foster child whose mother had died, recalled, "The Center was all my life. Going to the Edna Martin Christian Center and just sharing. It was always fun." Cutler, who later helped direct the Soul Ark, a Center program that worked with teenage boys, affirmed that his foster mother and Edna Martin taught him most of what he learned of value in his life. Both persuaded him to continue in his ministerial studies.[18]

Cutler remembered how poor the people in the neighborhood were as he was growing up. He lived on Massachusetts Avenue, what people called Fish Worm Alley, from Tenth Street up to Thirtieth Street. "As kids we would hustle customers for selling worms. Every other house sold worms, and we were wholesalers. In other words, we would go out at night and pick up the worms, and we would sell them to the sellers so that we could get a half a cent, two night crawlers for a penny; and in return they would sell them for twenty-five, thirty cents a dozen. So, not much profit, but it was big business."

One time Cutler saw the governor. "I believe the name was Craig . . . came through there, and had the cars with the running board, and we would get on the running board, put our arms through the window and point to the house wherever we work for a lady by the name of Mrs. Hughes, and say 'Stop right here,' pointing . . . she was the biggest retailer [of worms] in the neighborhood."

Cutler remembers that there were some "really rotten" kids that came to the Center. When they misbehaved, Edna would spank them, and if that did not work, she would put them out until they could come back and behave. It did not seem to matter how bad the kids were, Cutler said, they would not harm Edna. "I believe the kids would really fight if anybody thought about harming Mrs. Martin, because she fed them when they were hungry, clothes, whatever they needed, they could not get from home, and plenty of love, they would always get it from Dr. Martin."

Edna drew adults as well as children into her circle of care. "She filled a vacancy in . . . people's lives in general, many times frustrated women with families, single parents, really frustrated at the edge, not knowing where to go, would go and see her and leave feeling better." "She had faith . . . she was a praying woman . . . she would make you feel that you were so important, make you so relaxed that you would not mind spilling and sharing the whole problem. . . . She would sit there sometimes for a minute or two and she would just think and then she would start sharing what she felt the situation was going to be and, ten times out of ten [it would be that way]."[19]

The New Bethel Missionary Baptist Church that was next door to the Center has a long history of witness to the community. But Rev. George Baltimore, who was pastor when the Center was started,[20] did not approve of Edna or her work. Although he had originally agreed with the All Baptist Fellowship's decision that Edna could run a children's center in that location, he soon changed his mind. Baltimore's turnaround was based on gender rules in the black church. Since before the turn of the twentieth century, a bias existed in the Black Baptist Convention movement in which male ministers expected women to be silent helpmates.[21] Baltimore was an older man and still possessed that bias. In his opinion Edna did not understand the rules of how black women, especially black churchwomen, were supposed to submit to the authority of a black preacher. Edna, although a gentle woman with a loving spirit, was not meek and mild. She could be strong willed and outspoken.

Baltimore was not alone in his opposition to women playing dominant roles in the church. Vestiges of that bias still exist, and not just in the black community. According to Celestine Pettrie, a neighbor of Edna's, "Many of the ministers in the black community did not appreciate Edna's success, feeling that she was taking money away from programs that should have been run out of their churches. The fact that she was a woman only added fuel to the fire. But Edna was reaching children that the churches were not trying to reach."[22]

CHAPTER EIGHT

Solid Faith in a Shaky House

The building on Martindale was condemned, either by New Bethel Missionary Baptist Church's decision to expand its facilities, or by city action. By 1949 the East Side Christian Center Board of Directors purchased a site at 1537 North Arsenal Avenue, behind the Martindale address. The board later purchased two additional lots for a playground area. As Edna's work moved to the Arsenal site, a new pastor at New Bethel instituted a different ministry to the neighborhood. A newspaper article described the program as "providing food and clothing for the destitute, securing jobs for the unemployed, relieving mothers of the care of small children so they can hold jobs and providing a number of other services."[1] Perhaps Edna's absence next door had triggered the church's new ministry. However, there was more than enough work to be done in the neighborhood, and children poured into Edna's new program just down the alley.

Celestine D. Pettrie recalled Edna's success. "At the time Edna was at the Arsenal address, I was attempting to start a youth center for the Indianapolis Parks Department at

By 1949 the East Side Christian Center had moved to 1537 North Arsenal Avenue.

Lockefield Gardens [the city's first slum clearance project designed to provide apartment homes for black families]. No matter how hard I tried, I just was not having success. I told Edna, 'The reason you are so successful is that your program is Christ-centered and mine is Society-centered.'"[2]

In spite of opposition from church leaders in the black community, Edna was living her dream, albeit through a white world. In spring 1946 she attended the Missions Conference in the pastoral setting of the Northern Baptist Assembly at Green Lake, Wisconsin.[3] The conference was rich with inspirational messages, and the keynote address was on "The Christian and Race." Edna was inspired by such distinguished leaders as Dr. Edwin Bell of the American Baptist Foreign Mission Society in Europe; Dr. W. O. Lewis, general secretary of the Baptist World Alliance; and Dr. Luther Wesley Smith, president of the Northern Baptist Convention (which would become the American Baptist Churches USA).

Missionaries, wearing the costumes of the countries in which they served, participated in a "Festival of Light" pageant.

Edna, representing the East Side Christian Center, was a part of that moving procession. At the closing service the delegates walked in silence down the hill from the stately Roger Williams Inn to the "Point" jutting out into the lake. The only light on the grounds left shining was the cross on Judson Tower, the reflection of which sparkled and spread across the dark waters of Green Lake. Each person seemed to be standing at the foot of the widening, rippling cross.[4]

As a young girl, Edna had dreamed of following in the footsteps of Lulu Fleming, who was the first African-American woman to serve on a mission field. Now Edna's field was not Africa but the inner city of Indianapolis. Edna, with perhaps not even a high school education, but with considerable skills learned from the Willing Workers Class at Mount Zion Missionary Baptist Church, and an inner strength and desire, had become part of the worldwide mission outreach of the Northern Baptist Convention.

Although her mission field was in the black community, Edna spent most of her time in the white community, fundraising and educating Baptist church members about the work of the Center. It soon became apparent that Edna was a born ambassador. It did not matter to her whether the people were black or white. She treated everyone as special, and as coworkers would say, "She met no strangers, only neighbors."[5]

Carrie Bell Brown, the former director of the Dayton Christian Center, heard of Edna's work when she was a student at Baptist Missionary Training School in Chicago. Brown, a young Gullah woman, came to the school from her home on St. Helena Island, South Carolina. The Gullah, who may have begun coming to the outer banks of South Carolina as early as the sixteenth century, are the only group of Africans who have been able directly to trace their roots across the Atlantic to the villages of Sierra Leone in West Africa. They maintained their culture of rice agriculture, cast-net fishing, and arts and crafts such as coiled basketry. Brown's family (Bell) was descended from those Sierra Leone slaves.[6]

The Woman's Missionary Society of the American Baptist Convention provided scholarship funds for Brown's education. Before coming to Dayton, Brown ministered in the Christian centers at Peoria, Illinois, and Buffalo, New York. At the Dayton Christian Center, her work was very similar to Edna's program in Indianapolis.

"She was my mentor," Brown related. "There could never be another Edna Martin. Her graciousness, her love, her determination, her commitment just made her shine. Everyone just wanted to be in her presence."[7]

The All Baptist Fellowship disbanded in the early 1950s after providing an increasingly stable base of financial support and a growing sense of authenticity to the Center's work. The white Indianapolis Baptist Association took over the sponsorship of the Center alone. It was the resolve of the newly elected, twenty-four-member board of the Center, half white and half black, "to conduct a Christian social settlement house program," teach God's word, and develop Christian values among children and adults. Furthermore, the Center would serve "all people, regardless of race or creed."[8]

President of the board was Dr. U. S. Clutton, pastor of Tuxedo Park Baptist Church on the near east side. Vice president was Rev. Floyd Smith, pastor of Emmanuel Baptist Church; secretary was Rev. R. A. Muterspaugh, executive minister of the Indianapolis Baptist Association; and treasurer was B. J. Jackson, manager of Peoples Funeral Home.

Chairmen included Rev. William O. Breedlove, pastor of Calvary Baptist Church, a well-established church in the Brightwood area; Mrs. James H. Miller, an active member of First Baptist Church, which was then located downtown next to the World War Memorial on the northeast corner of Meridian and Vermont Streets; and Dr. O. K. Behrens, a First Baptist Church layman, who was an Eli Lilly and Company chemist.

First Baptist Church was an important connection for the Center's work because of the status that the historic church, built in 1822, held in the affairs of the city and other institutions such as the Church Federation. In the early 1960s, the congregation of First Baptist, along with the congregation of Second Presbyterian Church on the opposite corner, moved to the far north side as a result of the expansion of the World War Memorial property.

It would be the white Baptist community that molded Edna's ministry and image. Rev. Frank Alexander came from the Gateway Christian Center in Muncie to direct the work of the Center after Edna died. He later became pastor of Oasis of Hope Baptist Church at Twenty-fifth and Ralston, an influential church in the black community. He stressed the significance of her split commitment: "It was the success of Edna's contacts in the white community that catapulted her forward and made her different from others who were doing the same kind of work in the black community."[9]

Edna's working relationship with the white community also made her a virtual outcast in the religious and social hierarchy of the black community. In their study of the black church in the African-American experience, C. Eric Lincoln and Lawrence H. Mamiya concluded that the black church is the most economically independent institutional sector in the black community. "It does not depend upon white trustees to raise funds, for example, as do most of the black colleges. Nor does it depend upon white patronage to pay its pastors or erect its buildings."[10] So, in essence, Edna was going against the grain of traditional black church practices.

If Edna had been doing her charitable work just as a member of the Willing Workers Class at Mount Zion, which she was; or as a member of a woman's club, which she was; or associated with the women's wing of the National Baptist Convention, which she was; or if her work had only been in the black community and supported by the black community, she would have been hailed for her accomplishments. But she was not a "race woman," a term used to describe those whose contributions were mainly to the black race. The black community admires race women.

Edna knew the biblical admonitions about serving two masters. She constantly had to walk the line between not just two worlds, but three—the disenfranchised minority she served; the status church community where she worshiped but where she was not always accepted for her efforts at the Center; and the enfranchised white community she depended upon to support her work. She may not have been a race woman, but she had race pride. The fact that she was not accepted for her work in the black community no doubt caused her great pain at times. Edna's answer to the dilemma was simple—cling to the Rock. That response was her personal and public salvation. It could not always have been easy.

"Oreo" is a hurtful name in the black community, a name that describes someone who is black on the outside but white in the center. Although Edna was aware that some called her by that name, "blackness" was not the defining issue with her. She loved her blackness, but she glorified in her belief that she had been washed "white as snow, by the red blood of Jesus," and that was her definition.

"I know what it is like," Carrie Bell Brown recalled, thinking back to her Peoria, Brooklyn, and Dayton experiences working in the black communities yet sponsored mainly by white Baptists. She shook her head at the thought of the hurtful slur. "I've heard that from both blacks and whites. You just have to go on. You just can't let it stop you."[11]

"I love my color,"[12] Edna would frequently tell groups when the matter of race would come up. She made it clear that she was not bitter or ashamed of being black, although at times she would allude to being of mixed ancestry. When asked the usual cliché about what did she think of "races marrying," she would reply, "Races don't marry, people do."[13]

Whites that knew Edna, when they came to the Center, would in a rush of affection reach out and embrace her. Others, for whom blackness seemed to be an issue, would stand back with obvious reserve. "Aren't you going to come and give me a hug?" she would ask with a smile. "Come on," she would coax. Joshua Cutler remembered, "You would see the person reluctantly standing there, and then after they touch her, you see the person falling in love with her. That was just the kind of radiant personality she had."[14]

Frequently Edna would travel to rural and small-town Baptist churches scattered across Indiana—such as Warren, Scottsburg, Sullivan, Dana, and Waldron. In many of those places, blacks were not welcome in white churches or public places. She may have been the first African American that many in the Gosport First Baptist Church had ever worshiped with, but she charmed the congregation and won their hearts. One member, Julia Burns, became such a strong supporter of Edna's work that a house given to the Center would become the Julia Burns Homemaking Center.

Edna frequently visited the college town of Franklin, Indiana, from the mid-1940s to the 1960s, mainly to speak to groups related to the First Baptist Church, a supporting church of the East Side Christian Center. The members of First Baptist loved Edna, but the Franklin community was not a friendly place for blacks to visit or for that matter to live in during many of those years. On one occasion, after Edna spoke to a group at the First Baptist Church for an evening service, she walked the few blocks to the downtown bus station to wait for a coach back to Indianapolis. A man at the bus station informed her that she could not wait inside with the other passengers, and Edna was forced to wait outside in the pouring rain.[15]

During the late 1940s or early 1950s, Edna joined a group of Baptist women for lunch at a downtown Franklin cafeteria. When Edna entered the restaurant with the other women, the manager scurried to turn her away. The other women created such a storm of protest that the manager had little choice but to relent and serve Edna. The white women at First Baptist of Franklin were very indignant that the restaurant would not serve Edna, but at the same time, none of the black members of Second Baptist Church could have even entered those same restaurants.

Wanda Dunn and Martha Wales, African Americans who grew up in Franklin and who are participants in an oral history project for the Johnson County Historical Society, remember those days well. They both recall being warned by their parents not to enter restaurants in Franklin. Mostly it was an unwritten law, except for one restaurant where the sign in the window made it clear—NO BLACKS ALLOWED. "We just knew we would not be welcome," Dunn said. "It was easier to live in the South in some ways. There at least you knew what the laws were, but here in Franklin, much of the discrimination was accepted even if it was unlawful. It was just the way it was. Even though my mother and I worked in the kitchen of the Atterbury Restaurant [in downtown Franklin], we would not have entered the front door and asked to be served."[16]

"It was worse after the establishment of Camp Atterbury in 1941," Wales explained. "The community did not want all the black soldiers and their families in town. We rented rooms to them so they would have some place to live."[17]

Mary Alice Medlicott, archivist at the Franklin College Library, a lifelong resident of Franklin, and a member of First Baptist Church, explains, "We knew that it was wrong to discriminate, and our parents and church taught us to love and accept everyone, regardless of color, but I think most of the members felt rather helpless. They felt there was little they could do to change the social mores of the community."[18]

Dunn and Wales recall that the members of First Baptist Church helped out their church in a number of ways, even providing the bricks for the Second Baptist Church building. They and Medlicott remember times when the two churches would join together for fellowship.

"It was just hard for the message of love and acceptance to carry over into everyday action," Medlicott said. "But Edna

Martin tried to help us see that it was our Christian duty to love one another and cross racial barriers."[19]

During a Baptist women's conference at Washington, Indiana, Edna again was confronted by restaurant management and asked to leave. Without any argument or making the situation known to the other women, she quietly excused herself and slipped out. Later she told the women, "When the Spirit is ready it will move, but until that time I have enough Christian grace that it doesn't bother me. There will be another day and sooner or later it [the Spirit] will win."[20]

At churches such as those in Warren, Sardinia, Petersburg, Boggstown, Milan, and Camby, the women would become her devoted advocates, conscientiously contributing money, articles of clothing and quilts, and time to the work. Many churches named a missionary circle after Edna Martin.

One morning Edna was mulling over the problem that there were numerous families around the Center who had no food. She picked up her telephone and contacted a group of Baptist

Edna Martin Christian Center Archives

Edna Martin depended on the support of the white community—particularly the women from Baptist churches, who supplied money, clothing, food, and volunteer work to keep things running at the Center.

women who had worked with her on other projects and shared the need with them. Thirteen women immediately came to the Center. Edna explained, "We mapped out a program whereby we would put food on the table of those families at six o'clock every evening. Over a period of time, each woman cooked a pot of food on her specific day and brought it to the Center."[21]

Many urban churches as well as small-town churches supported the work. Some of the strongest supporters were white churches who served white neighborhoods that were not far removed from poverty themselves. Dr. U. S. Clutton, pastor of Tuxedo Park Baptist Church, was eager to tell how his experiences with Edna had changed his social consciousness and his sense of the family of Christ. He felt that she had affected many in his white blue-collar congregation in the same way.

From the poor and rich alike, Edna gained friends. Neighbors on Arsenal Avenue would frequently see the expensive car of Edith Stokely Moore, daughter of the founder of the Stokely Brothers and Company that moved its operations from Tennessee to Indianapolis in 1944, pull up in front of the Center. Moore, a member of Crooked Creek Baptist Church, would spend the day sorting clothes. She supported the Center work as long as she lived, serving on the board of directors many years. The Center received several grants from the Stokely and Moore foundations.

Woodruff Place Baptist Church, down the street on East Michigan from the large, historic campus of Arsenal Technical High School, was always active in support of the Center. Along with the Central Baptist Association, Woodruff Place formed the twenty-eight-member Christian Friendliness Club, organized to encourage support of the Center by other Baptist churches. With the addition of members from Greenwood Baptist Church, Galveston Baptist Church, and others, the club multiplied many times over the years.

Edna's faith left no room for worry or doubt. Paying off the debt on the Arsenal Avenue site was a matter of urgent concern for

Center board members, but not for Edna. "God will provide," was her mantra. The money came in from black and white churches, individuals all over the state, and from American Baptists in other states, with the final amount coming in 1955 from a loan of $5,100 from Mr. and Mrs. Louis Rainey of Lebanon, Indiana.

Although at the beginning of her career Edna ran counter to the authority of a local pastor, she soon made it very clear that she did not want to compete with the ministers in the community. She refused to have worship services on Sunday morning and evening so people would be encouraged to attend a church in the neighborhood.

There were times though when Edna felt that the neighborhood black churches "have been lax in witnessing in the manner that they should," as far as support of her work.[22] Several times in 1958, because of repair bills or the result of break-ins, the financial reports were showing constant deficits. Edna urged the board to make an appeal directly to the "Negro people in Indianapolis, asking for contributions for the general expenses of the Center."[23] She thought if she could reach those not involved with the established black churches, she might get a better response. However, Edna knew that many of the smaller black churches were struggling to keep their doors open and pay staff and expenses.

Rev. L. Eugene Ton, former executive minister of the American Baptist Churches of Indiana, said, "She would literally pound on doors," trying to get support from black pastors in the area. "Generally, they would respond to her personally and perhaps give some aid in the form of food or materials, but it was seldom a wholehearted effort. In time, many of the pastors would come to respect Edna, but they would never really give her their stamp of approval."[24]

Some of the black pastors and churches faithfully supported the Center in various ways, especially those associated with the All Baptist Fellowship. Some of those included Rev. J. T. Highbaugh, Rev. F. F. Young, Rev. David C. Venerable, Rev.

Walter D. Edwards, Rev. James Williams, and Dr. Andrew J. Brown. Other supporters were New Hope Baptist Church, New Bethel Missionary Baptist Church (under Dr. F. Benjamin Davis), and St. John Missionary Baptist Church.[25]

Rosa Lee Brown, the college-educated wife of Dr. Andrew J. Brown, was like a daughter to Edna. "When we first came to the city and Andrew was assistant at Mount Zion, before we started at St. Johns, I met Edna. I was very insecure then, just a young pastor's wife in a strange city and neighborhood, much different from my home in Chicago. I was lacking in self-values. Edna restored my sense of personal worth. She convinced me that I had a calling just like my husband's. She educated me in the thought that women could have a calling to minister just like men. She helped my husband in this sense as well."[26]

One Presbyterian church faithfully supported the Center—Witherspoon Presbyterian Church, a mainly black congregation at 436 West Twenty-fifth Street. The church was located near the Martins' home, and Edna likely sought out its pastor, Rev. Clinton Marsh. During Edna's childhood and young adult life, members of Witherspoon church, especially the women, were activists in the community, and Edna had not forgotten their lessons in Christian service and compassion. She was always grateful for their love and support.[27]

Edna loyally supported the black churches, continuing to be active at Mount Zion, in its women's program, and in the work of the larger National Baptist Convention. Perhaps more importantly, she sent hundreds of children who had come to profess Christ during Center programs into the care of neighborhood churches.

Even though her own community assistance was sporadic, Edna's faith, good works, and firm stand reached many in city government, including the Marion County Juvenile Court. When an unusually bad, defiant, and seemingly incorrigible boy would come before the juvenile judges, Edna would say, "I want that boy." Moreover, the judges, who knew the miracles she could work, would release the boy to her care.

This practice of releasing troubled youth to Christian agencies was not unusual during this time. The Juvenile Aid Division of the Indianapolis Police Department cooperated on a regular basis with the Church Federation in handling cases. According to a study, in a seven-month period during 1948, the police department referred 876 children to the Church Federation, which in turn referred the children to 217 different churches located throughout the city.[28]

Judge Harold Fields became a friend and admirer of Edna. Her word was law with him when it came to releasing a boy or girl from custody.[29] On one occasion, she had difficulty with a boy who was in trouble in juvenile court. She reportedly called the boy into her office and took the strap to him. When they went to the court sometime afterwards, Judge Field reportedly asked her, "What did you do to that boy to straighten him up?" Edna replied, "I merely gave him what he was asking for all along."[30]

According to a study made in the 1950s of the neighborhood

Edna Martin Christian Center Archives

Members from American Baptist churches bring clothes to the Sales House on Arsenal Avenue, where Edna and her sister, Thelma Herrington, greet them.

of the Center, delinquency rates had dropped substantially in the neighborhood. It would continue to do so up into the 1960s, although it would still be higher than other parts of the city.[31] Edna would be given credit for much of that improvement, along with friend, neighbor, and sometimes called "competitor," Father Bernard Strange of St. Rita's Catholic Church, then at the 1800 block of North Arsenal Avenue. Father Strange, although white, was considered "one of us" by his parishioners and instituted many programs for the families of the community.[32]

One key to building pride in the youth and families of the community was providing decent clothing. Sometimes Edna would have to remind the contributing churches not to send ragged articles or mismatched shoes. Because she was always diplomatic, her admonishment did not offend her supporters. Always accentuating the positive, she would remind donors how important it was for children and families to have warm and suitable clothing that would help them build self-esteem. It was very important to black children and parents not to be dirty or shabby. Not forgetting to do her own part to build responsibility in the distribution of clothing, Edna asked those who could to pay a nominal fee for articles, "as a matter of self-respect."[33]

Indiana Baptists were learning from Edna. She was confronting them in her own Spirit-filled way with the heart of the Gospel, and they were listening. She would prompt her white audiences to ask of themselves regarding the plight of the black community, "What does this condition mean to the Church, to Christians? What kind of gospel do we preach and teach? Who is our neighbor and where is our neighborhood?"

Edna described "a slum" as any place where there was little hope, little concern, little respect, and little opportunity. She would never leave a meeting without gently chiding those who had been present that the people she served were children of God. "God made them, just like He made you and me."[34]

Programming Around the Rock

Taking her lead from the organization and format of the programs at Mount Zion Missionary Baptist Church, Edna Martin organized the work at the East Side Christian Center around departments: Nursery, Primary, and a little later, Junior, Teen, and Adult. Each department had several programs, and overwhelming numbers of the Martindale community attended.

Continuing the celebratory dedication of a new building addition in March, holiday parties in December 1954 saw hundreds of boxes of food, toys, and clothing brought to the Center, mainly by Indiana Baptist women. Each little girl received a character doll and each boy a billfold. That was no easy feat as several hundred children were enrolled in the programs. Edna was probably pleased with the gifts of several Singer sewing machines and metal filing cabinets.[1]

She reported that "one of the best years in the history of the Center" was in 1955, "with five morning classes, 600 hot meals served, 26 conversions, and a Vacation [Bible] School of 189 for two weeks closing with a picnic at Riverside Amusement Park with 200 attending."[2]

During April 1958, twenty-four hundred people attended Center programs. All the events reinforced the ideas of self-esteem and a "Christian way of life." The singing of "America the Beautiful" and the pledges to the Christian and American flags and the Bible started each class. God and country were at the center of the program, and the pledges reinforced the ideas of brotherhood under one God.

After pledging allegiance to the American flag, the children would stand quietly, with their hands over their hearts and say: "I pledge allegiance to the Christian Flag and to the Savior for whose Kingdom it stands, one brotherhood uniting all mankind in service and in love." Turning to look down at a Bible on a table, they would recite: "I pledge allegiance to the Bible, God's Holy Word, and will make it a lamp unto my feet, a light unto my path, and hide its words in my heart that I may not sin against God." Inherent in Edna Martin's approach to teaching were the principals of citizenship and equality. "When you have done this," she said, speaking of the teaching of faith, clean living, and allegiance to country, "you have done something for all of Indianapolis."[3]

Arts and crafts were an important and fun part of all the programs, and Edna was very creative in the use of cast-offs in the crafts projects. Once, after a telephone repairman discarded wire, she collected the various colored strands and wove a multi-colored basket. Satisfied with the product, she called Indiana Bell and asked if they would send leftover wire to the Center so that the children could learn basket weaving.[4]

Edna never wasted anything—leftover wire or lives. Rev. Louis Nelson, who was the Minister of Mission Support for the American Baptist Churches of Indiana and Indianapolis, remembers one day when the two of them were on a speaking tour. They had stopped for lunch and Edna had finished her cup of hot tea. Nelson noticed that she took the wet tea bag, wrapped it in a napkin, and placed it in her purse. She must have seen him looking at her endeavor. "There's a lot of good

Children on the playground at the Arsenal Avenue East Side Christian Center. Play was important to Edna. The board of directors of the Center purchased two additional lots next to the building on Arsenal for a playground area.

left in that tea bag," she explained.[5]

Vacation Bible School for ages three to fifteen was one of the first programs offered at the Center. Teachers taught hundreds of scriptures from each of the Old and New Testaments and had chapter and verse quizzes on them. Edna and the staff would choose verses to show the children their place in relation to God. One often-repeated scripture was, "Whosoever shall do the will of God, the same is my brother, my sister and mother." Another was, "Ye shall receive power, after the Holy Ghost is come upon you."[6]

In 1955 the Vacation Bible School closed with a picnic at Riverside Amusement Park. During this time Riverside Park was segregated and blacks were admitted only one day a year. It is unclear whether the children went on the "Negro Day"; however, Rev. Ed Dowdy, pastor of the Woodruff Place Baptist Church, used the church bus to transport two hundred to the picnic at the park.[7]

Edna saw play as an opportunity for health and moral development, so she made sure playground equipment was purchased for the Center. The children delighted in games such as 4-Square and "trash-can" basketball, which required little equipment.

At one time Mary French, a home economics teacher supplied by the Indianapolis Public Schools, taught sewing and cooking classes. On Wednesdays and Thursdays mothers in the neighborhood repaired clothing or made items including pillowcases, clothing, or quilts. Quilting was not only an activity that yielded accomplishment, it also afforded time for fellowship and helped to create a sense of mutual support among the women.

Mildred Majors had been brought to Indianapolis as a two year old from North Carolina and raised by an aunt and an uncle, who was a Pullman porter. She attended Crispus Attucks High School and Indiana University, Indianapolis campus. It was to Edna and the Center though that she turned to help raise her four children in the Martindale area. She remembers

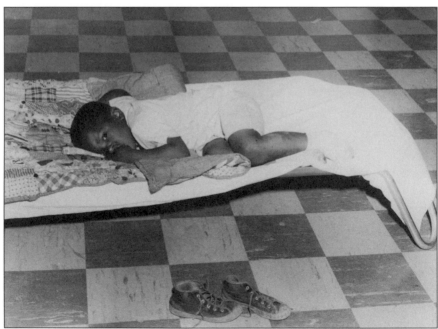

Edna Martin Christian Center Archives

Edna often served as a mediator between "her children" and school officials. She explained the conditions the children lived under and the many obstacles they had to overcome.

Edna as a sweet person who could be strong and stern when she needed to be. "She would make those children mind. I would go and help at the Sales House and in other ways."[8] Mildred's youngest son Michael remembers those days at the Center—the games, the playground, the meals. Nobody had to wonder where the kids were in the neighborhood if they weren't home, for they were all at the Center with Edna. As Michael remembers, "Mrs. Martin took care of us there. There really is no place like that now for kids."[9]

There was not time or money to do many things on Edna's agenda. Her concerns not only centered on the Center and its programs, but also reached across the block to the public school. School 26 was the school that most of the Center's children attended. Edna became unhappy with some of the teachers at School 26 because she felt that they belittled the children because of their clothes or their poor language skills. As a result, Edna became an active member of the school's Parent-Teacher Association, serving as a buffer between "her children" and school officials. She would explain, "You must understand the conditions under which these children live and the obstacles, besides clothes, they have to overcome." She pleaded for compassion.

The walls of the house on Arsenal Avenue were bulging. The staff, which included Vivian Simmons, Hobson Zeigler, Delores Mitchell, Thelma Herrington, Elizabeth McDonald, Thelma Paragon, and Rev. Willard R. Jewell,[10] was overextended. The Center's board searched to find a qualified program director to help the dedicated staff, but none had been found that Edna would accept. The treasurer would sigh with relief if there was even a balance of $35.71,[11] instead of dipping discouragingly into the red. The neighborhood was changing, and, as Edna would say, the Kingdom of God was growing.

Tested and Tried and Found Wanting

Directing the East Side Christian Center work, raising funds and support for its operation, and involving herself in community affairs took their toll on Edna Martin's health. In May 1952, over a period of three weeks, she lost twenty pounds. Of course, she would never admit that she was not feeling well. "Oh, I'm fine, just a little tired," she would smile. "Just don't you worry."

Her friends did worry. They knew it would be almost impossible to get her to slow down, so they did the next best thing— gave her wheels. Sixty-five friends gave love gifts, the largest $75 and the smallest $1, amounting to $647. Along with Hedges Pontiac's discount, and the Sigler Insurance Agency's cooperation, they presented her with a good used car.[1]

Not all of Edna's relationships with the leaders of the Indianapolis Baptist Association were loving or smooth. Some of the executives and pastors found it easier to work with Edna on a project in the black community than others did. Oftentimes this was because many of them had had little contact with blacks before.

It seemed especially hard for Indianapolis Association Executive Secretary Rev. Richard Muterspaugh to accept Edna's way of doing things and to work with her to accomplish her vision of ministry for the program. Many times they tried each other's patience. Their styles were different as was their vision of the Center mission, but their purpose was the same, to see the ministry flourish. Many in the American Baptist community would give Muterspaugh credit for the construction of the new building on Caroline Avenue in 1964.[2]

In 1957 the Center's work came under the scrutiny of executives at the American Baptist Home Mission Society (now known as National Ministries) as a result of some criticism of its operation. The board of directors approved a study to review the program. The reviewer, Edward D. Rapp of the Home Mission Society, concluded that even though the Center was Christian in nature, there needed to be a better balance of secular and religious instruction. He reported, "A well rounded balanced program of religious and secular is necessary for each child to grow properly and to receive the values that might accrue from such a good balance."[3]

Rapp further suggested that the Center contact the State Department of Public Health and the State Department of Public Welfare and work toward meeting the requirements for a licensed nursery school. He felt it was "unchristian" to permit the program to exist under conditions that were not healthy and safe. This was done, and the Center was licensed for forty-eight children.

One especially interesting portion of the study had to do with Rapp's evaluation of Edna Martin. He summarized that Edna reserved "all the important decisions for herself to make," and that the program supervisors "should be given more freedom in working with the teachers." Rapp also suggested that Edna "be freed of some detail work in order to take some training in administration in order to strengthen the total overall administrative picture" of the Center.[4]

As for the staff, Rapp objected on the grounds that few had college degrees, although most had gained experience from

Edna Martin Christian Center Archives

Edna Martin in her office at the Arsenal Avenue Center location.

teaching in church-related programs. "The teaching staff has necessarily had to be recruited from those who either have missionary devotion or because of lack of training [have] not been able to get full-time teaching jobs. Few people on the staff are fully trained for their job," he wrote. Rapp also noted that none of the teachers had any kind of social work background or experience in the social work or casework field.[5] What Rapp did not mention was that the staff was woefully underpaid.

Rapp, in his 1957 report, summarized:

The population is largely colored with a scattering of whites here and there. The influx in population usually comes from the South and is quite possibly the first stop for many of the Southern Rural folk on the way to the North. Eye-witnesses class the newcomers as usually of a lower economic and cultural background. According to these same eyewitnesses' accounts, however, a goodly number of people remain in the community, establishing a solid core of individuals with a fairly good economic background.

Since 1952, the school population in School #26 has steadily grown. This is some indication that the population in the community has also grown, however this is difficult to establish statistically. According to the school officials there is a great deal of mobility among school children and a great deal of turnover in the school population. This is to say that school children move in and out quite rapidly. This indicates something of the mobility of households and families within the community.

The area which the Center serves [bounded by Tenth Street on the south, College Avenue on the west, by Thirtieth Street on the north and by Rural Street on the east] is contained within the railroad tracks North, West, and South, and the better residential section immediately to the East. Great numbers of children come from this area and families are being reached through these children. Housing is generally bad to slum, with sanitary conditions sub-standard. A great many delinquency cases still come from the area. Illegitimacy and Aid to Dependent Children probably account for the greater areas of welfare service. No other agencies are projecting service to the area at the present time. Socially, culturally, and economically the area is below standard. A great many new people, coming from the south, are moving into the already overcrowded housing. It is very definitely an area of continued service for the East-side Christian Center.[6]

In a spirit of honest amazement, Rapp admitted, "The building is old, the program space is too small, the equipment is minimal and yet, the Center is doing a tremendous job with the children and families in the community."[7]

Edna accepted the criticism. At least, she did not vocally protest; although it must have pained her that anyone would think she was not worthy to lead her beloved Center. For Edna, it was a difficult time—she and her work had been tested and tried and found wanting.

Edna Martin Christian Center Archives

The Sales House and the East Side Christian Center on 1500 Arsenal Avenue.

She told the Home Mission Society that she was willing to take training in administration, which she did to some extent by attending National Laboratory School Conferences, held at the Children's Center at Green Lake, Wisconsin, a four-year summer course. Edna worked there with teachers, ministers, and Sunday school superintendents from all around the nation, observing children and members of the highly trained staff in the newest Christian education methods.

It was no secret to her staff or to the members of the board that Edna's strong point was not administration. People were her interest, not paper. Although the staff at times felt stifled in their opportunities for creative input, they still loved their leader. As one staff member said, "Mrs. Martin had our respect, obedience and love. I treasure all the time I was so blessed to walk in her shadow."[8]

Edna increasingly tried to provide training for her staff, sending them to pre-school conferences at Green Lake, Purdue University, Butler University, and other sites. She began visiting other Christian centers—such as the Dayton (Ohio)

Christian Center and the Weirton Christian Center in West Virginia. There were not enough resources to send as many staff members as she would have liked.

By 1958 nine members of the teaching staff had some college training, and not all were Baptists. Rev. Samuel Wright, pastor of Scott Methodist Church, a graduate of Lincoln University in Jefferson City, Missouri, and Garrett Biblical Institute in Evanston, Illinois, taught eight- and nine-year-old boys part time. Thelma Paragon, a member of Simpson Methodist Church and a graduate of Blaker's Teachers College, taught in the girls' program.

There was so much to do, so many children to reach, and so little time and resources.

CHAPTER ELEVEN

A Closer Look at the Harvest Field

In 1962 Larry A. Rood, a member of Edna Martin's staff and an Indianapolis area resident who had a B.A. in sociology from Indiana Central College (later the University of Indianapolis), decided to do a study of the East Side Christian Center community. His brother Jon Rood had served on the staff, and Larry had a personal interest in the work. Rood had assistance from Lawrence Voyles, assistant director, Marion County Department of Public Welfare; Father Bernard Strange of St. Rita Catholic Church; Francis Schmidt, director of the Indianapolis PAL Clubs; John Mascare, assistant city engineer; Barton Anson, Chief Probation Officer, Marion County Juvenile Court; Evelyn McCanon, director of extensions, the Indianapolis Public Library; James White of the Indianapolis Redevelopment Commission; the Indianapolis Police Department; and Center volunteers.[1]

His sample population was an area bounded by Twenty-first Street on the north, the Monon Railroad on the west, Roosevelt Avenue on the south, and Roosevelt and Hillside Avenues on the east. The random sample was every fourth dwelling. Of the houses sampled, he found 22 vacant, 12 where residents refused to give information, 20 where no one was at home, and 164 where the survey was completed.

A summary of his report revealed that the educational level of the residents was almost "three years below that for the rest of Indianapolis." Reasons included a lack of jobs requiring skilled labor for blacks; a large number of residents coming from the South, where the education of black children was oftentimes far inferior to that of whites; and crowded housing that made studying, especially for high school students, almost impossible.[2]

The housing problem was both qualitative and quantitative; there was not enough housing and what there was often did not meet even the most minimum standards. The report indicated that 99.4 percent of the residences were built before 1939. Of the 4,808 homes in the area, "38.5% were owner-occupied, with the average cash value being $6,500. The average value for owner-occupied homes for the city over-all was $11,500." In the area 67 percent had one bathroom, 3 percent had more than one, and 30 percent either shared a bathroom with another family or had none at all. Crowding was another problem, with 47 percent of the homes having more than 1.1 persons per room, usually many more than that.[3]

In tract 530, where the Center was located, the median income after taxes was $2,133, and the median annual rent was $792, or 37 percent of the net income. Breaking that down, a median size family in this area of 3.3 persons had weekly, after taxes and rent, $28.78 to live on.

Most residents of the community were adopted Hoosiers, 71 percent having come from other states, the majority from the South, mainly from Kentucky and Tennessee. It appeared that people who moved into the area kept on moving with a high degree of mobility.

As for public welfare, the study area had 39 Old Age Assistance (OAA) cases, while the average tract for the county had 13.8. For Aid to Dependent Children (ADC), the average number of recipients per census tract in Marion County was 10.4 while the average number of cases per tract in the study area was 57.

The Indianapolis Police Department's Car 24 patrolled the area bordered by Tenth, College, Twenty-first, and Rural. It was ranked "one of the busiest cars in the city." There were 1,053 reported crimes against persons in Indianapolis in 1961, with the share of an average district being 35. Car 24's area had 72, or over twice the average for the city. For the city, 9,506 crimes against property were reported, of which 475 were in the Car 24 area, nearly half again that of the city average.

The study stated that "the national average for juveniles who become involved in delinquent acts was between one and two per cent of the total juvenile population. For the tracts involved in the study, the percentages range from four to seven per cent, many times that of the national average." One possible cause of this high delinquency rate might have been in juvenile court cases that were not the fault of the children. "From the study area in 1961 there were sixty-three neglected children who had either to be placed in foster homes or in an institution because their families abandoned all responsibility toward them."[4] Such cases were processed through the juvenile court and could account for the higher ratings in the area.

Income and employment were serious problems in the community. "Within the study area, the average percentage of the labor force unemployed at the 1960 census was 10.0%, while the average for the city of Indianapolis was 4.1%. The median percentage of non-white unemployment for Indianapolis was 7.6 percent."[5] While the median household income in Indianapolis was $6,609, median income for nonwhite households was $4,390, and for those households in the Center area it was $2,667.[6]

The neighborhood north of Massachusetts and east of Roosevelt and Hillside Avenues, commonly known as the Hillside area, was occupied by approximately two-thirds white

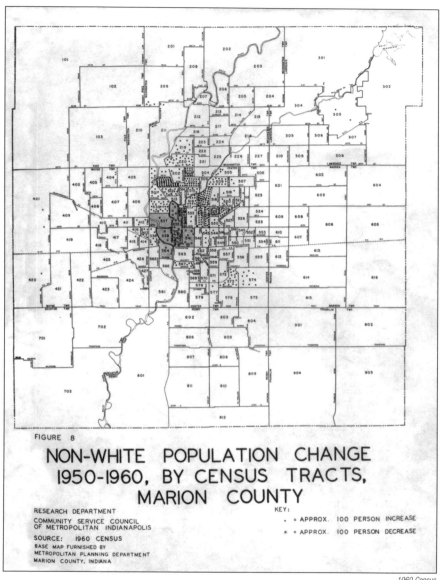

FIGURE 8

NON-WHITE POPULATION CHANGE 1950-1960, BY CENSUS TRACTS, MARION COUNTY

RESEARCH DEPARTMENT
COMMUNITY SERVICE COUNCIL
OF METROPOLITAN INDIANAPOLIS

SOURCE: 1960 CENSUS

BASE MAP FURNISHED BY
METROPOLITAN PLANNING DEPARTMENT
MARION COUNTY, INDIANA

KEY:

. = APPROX. 100 PERSON INCREASE

* = APPROX. 100 PERSON DECREASE

1960 Census

Nonwhite population changes 1950–1960, Marion County.

residents and one-third nonwhite residents, according to the 1960 census. This area jumped 458 percent in black occupancy between 1950 and 1960, and evidence would indicate that this trend would continue.

According to the report, "Interstate 70 will be a direct

access route to the central city from the northeast. It follows a path down roughly a block to a block and a half north of Massachusetts Avenue. It will take a few feet of the southeast corner of the Center playground. Also, it will wipe out nearly all of the area which the Center draws from to the south, involving probably a little less than one-third of the children who came to the Center."[7]

It was noted that a highway such as this would provide "a natural 'community barrier' making it impossible for anyone living on the other side to attend Center activities. Thus, the Center will be placed at the bottom of a neighborhood instead of in the center of it. In addition, parents might tend to be hesitant to send their children to an institution located this close to such a highway. Highway noise would be one more factor to take into consideration."[8]

As the report noted, "Other road improvements planned were the development of Sixteenth Street and Martindale Avenue into primary streets, with four lanes open to traffic at all times. Thus these streets also could be expected to form 'community barriers,' especially for the smaller children."[9]

As a result of Rood's study, more attention was given to the connection of the Center's work to the problems of the greater whole of the city of Indianapolis. Local government agencies were made more aware of the Center's desire to be a partner in finding solutions to those problems.

A new adversary of the Center ministry arose from the charts and graphs of the Metropolitan Development Commission—not crime, or juvenile delinquency, poverty, or even apathy, but an enemy of steel and concrete—Interstate 70.

CHAPTER TWELVE

Rich Men, Good Gifts, and Blind Faith

Edna Martin's "blind faith" built the new Caroline Avenue facility. If God could "call her out" to use a fourteen-dollar-a-month room, rat-infested house, and a cramped to overflowing, decrepit building, why wouldn't God provide a fine, new facility for His purposes? In addition to Edna's faith, the beautiful facility would be built with monies raised by Indiana Baptists, contributions from the American Baptist Home Mission Society, and generous grants from the Lilly Foundation; however, before that building could become a reality, certain things had to come about.

Despite an addition built in the early 1950s, the building on Arsenal Avenue was overcrowded with people and programs. Two thousand meals a month were served on a budget of one hundred dollars, another "loaves and fishes" miracle made possible only by the donations of churches, institutions, and individuals.[1]

By the 1960s, an average of five thousand people came through the East Side Christian Center on North Arsenal Avenue each month.[2] There were 799 children registered in the programs in 1964, and the championship Center adult basketball team played an all-star team and won, with the profits going to the Community Campaign.[3]

Rev. Paul Madinger, Center treasurer, sent out a dramatic appeal to Center supporters for a new building. He described sitting beside Edna's desk as she opened the drawer and shuddered as three or four bugs scampered across the papers that she was retrieving.

Madinger wrote:

We have three very old houses in an aged and decaying neighborhood of Indianapolis. Two of the houses have been joined by a hallway to provide greater use of the facilities for classes and other activities. Every day 50 to 60 hot meals are served to children attending the Center.

The wood is infested with termites. The staff must war constantly against bugs and rodents, with the condition of the building being on the side of the pests.

Last week Mrs. Martin told me, "We cover the mice holes and they just bore another hole right beside the one that is covered. And now," she continued, "we are being invaded by rats! They are big bold ones that run across the floor when we come to work in the mornings." In despair she added, "Mrs. Herrington won't open the closet where we keep the supplies because big rats have jumped out of it. I have to get the materials out for her each day."

But the bugs and the rats and the termites only point up the problem so obvious to all who drive down Arsenal Avenue: The Center Must Have New Building Facilities.

Upon entering any door of any building, one is immediately confronted with the need for space. Boxes of materials are stacked along the passageways for want of a better place to store them. Classes are held in areas through which people must pass. The office is located on what was once the small front porch of the house at 1537 where in the winter the small electric heater gives little protection against the cold.

Dining space, recreation space, classroom space, cooking

space, sleeping space (for toddlers' naps), storage space, salesroom space and office space are [beyond minimal].[4]

In May 1961 the board of directors and Indianapolis Baptist Association executive minister Rev. Richard Muterspaugh sought assistance and cooperation from the American Baptist Home Missionary Society and other avenues of support to build a new facility. Indiana Baptist women were among the first to contribute to the new building, followed by the Indiana Baptist Convention, with Dr. Dallas West as executive minister.

Some very influential people comprised the board that directed that new building. B. J. Jackson, manager of the Peoples Funeral Home, was outgoing chairman of the board. Jackson was succeeded by Rev. Floyd Smith of Emmanuel Baptist Church. Dr. Andrew J. Brown of St. John Missionary Baptist Church was vice chairman, and Edith Stokely Moore, the Stokely food family heir, was secretary. Others on the board

Edna Martin Christian Center Archives

The ground breaking for the new East Side Christian Center building on Caroline Avenue, 1946.

The American Baptist/Indiana News Section, *January 1971*

John S. Lynn, general manager of the Lilly Endowment Foundation, was touched by Edna's work. From 1964 to 1973, thanks in great part to Lynn, the Center received grants that made the construction of the Caroline Avenue facility possible.

included R. K. Smith, retired executive of the Senate Avenue YMCA, and Willa Owsley, a leader in the black community. However, it was the Lilly Endowment that brought Edna's dreams for a new building and new programs to reality.

One day a dignified, well-dressed stranger came in to observe the activities of the Center. That gentleman was John S. Lynn, director of the Lilly Endowment. He began a friendship with Edna that resulted in the beautiful new building at the corner of Caroline Avenue and Fernway, adjoining Oak Hill Park, not more than a mile from the Arsenal site.

Lynn recalled, "The first time I visited the Center, I just fell in love with her [Edna] and what she was doing." Lynn continued, "She was a great lady. So Christ-like."[5]

Lynn became general manager of the Lilly Endowment Foundation in 1962, and he determined that his chief interest was to locate projects that benefited the community and that exemplified free enterprise and private control, with limited government involvement. "Edna just fit the bill," Lynn said. Furthermore, the Christ-centered atmosphere of the woman and her work touched Lynn, and this was a deciding factor. "She did wonderful things at the Center. It was just such a pleasure for me to be able to deliver the checks to her. She became my friend and for a number of years attended a Bible study held in my home directed by my son."[6]

Lynn believes that it might have been Ruth Lilly, second wife of Eli Lilly, who originally brought Edna's work to the attention of the Lilly Endowment board. Ruth Lilly, well known for her interest in Christian charities, may have come across Edna's work by word of mouth or from referrals made to the fund. L. Eugene Ton, who was on the East Side Christian Center board at that time, believes it could have been Reverend Madinger or others on the board who sent in a request for a grant for the building. Then again, Dr. Otto K. Behrens, who was a Lilly chemist and a member of the board, could have passed the word along. However it came about,

Lynn became the key player.

For a nine-year period, from 1964 to 1973, the Center received $192,000 from Lilly Endowment because of the influence of Lynn. That money, plus contributions from Indiana Baptists and the American Baptist Home Mission Society, made the construction of the Caroline Avenue facility possible as well as the purchase and renovation of the Soul Ark, a facility used for boys' work programs.

According to *Eli Lilly: A Life, 1885–1977*, by James H. Madison, Lynn's support of projects such as the Center caused dismay among some in the Lilly management and others in the national philanthropic community. Lynn, a DePauw University and Harvard Business School graduate and the nephew of Charles Lynn, an early Lilly executive, "pushed his interest in the trinity of free markets, anti-communism, and fundamental Christianity"[7] as far as he could.

The endowment report for 1963 under Lynn claimed that philanthropy "should strengthen the foundation of liberty, which we interpret as including a belief in God and His Son Jesus Christ, a limited constitutional republic, the right to own property, and the freedom to engage in enterprises designed to maximize creative energies and their exchange."[8]

Lynn's sponsor in the Lilly family was not Eli but J. K. Lilly, who had been influenced by Barry Goldwater's book, *Conscience of a Conservative*. J. K., Lynn, and Behrens were all active in the Indianapolis YMCA as well as the Church Federation.[9] J. K. and Lynn had many similar interests and social philosophies.

Eli had a different attitude toward social change and the involvement of the church in the activities of the black community. In Madison's biography, he tells that Eli did not approve of the changing times of the 1960s, especially in regard to church and social and racial integration. A new rector at Eli's beloved Christ Church (Episcopal) on the Circle, Peter Lawson, replaced Dr. Paul Moore, Jr., in 1964. Moore made every effort to be sensitive and work within the bounds of most of his congregation including Eli Lilly. Lawson, in contrast, was more concerned with effecting change in the areas of social and racial integration.

John G. Rauch, Sr., a member of Christ Church and Eli's friend and personal attorney, warned Lawson that "he had to choose whether he would confine his activities to religious, theological, and philosophical objectives or to enter the political arena and engage in debate and agitations . . . such as public housing; juvenile delinquency; crime; racial integration."[10] This talk did not seem to deter the young dean and rector.

In theory, Eli accepted that the Christian thing to do in regard to racial integration was to support it. He did support charitable projects in the inner city in many ways including the Talbot Fund to establish housing; the Cathedral House program, a ministry situated in the inner city that opened in 1960 to serve the needs of neighborhood children; and the strong record of integration at Eli Lilly and Company during the 1950s. In practice, though, Eli was anxious about integration crossing the threshold of Christ Church. In personal notes he made in regard to his concern about his brash rector's views, Eli wrote, "I have not seen an objectional Negro in C[hrist] C[hurch]. . . . However we all know of numberless instances where neighborhoods and schools have been gradually infiltrated and taken over."[11] He advised that at Christ Church, "all recruitment efforts [for blacks] should be stopped."[12] He withdrew his financial support from the church he loved so much when his advice was not taken. The "hippie dean," as Eli described Lawson, was replaced with a new dean and rector who generally ascribed to Eli's wishes, and financial support again flowed to Christ Church.[13]

J. K. died in 1966. In 1972 a major study, *The Big Foundations*, written by Waldemar A. Nielsen, was published, criticizing the conservative approach of the Lilly Endowment. Eli's "initial reaction was anger"; however, he "admitted there had been embarrassing support for some organizations and too much negativism and hostility to government."[14] Soon after, Lynn left the Lilly Endowment.

It was not Lilly money alone that made the new building possible. Offerings from American Baptists and others across the nation helped pay for the facility. According to Rev. Richard Padrick, who served on the board during the construction of the new building, Indiana Baptists really wanted to raise funds for a larger, better-equipped building for the work, but Edna wanted just a small, simple structure. Being a humble person, she wanted to avoid any appearance of pretension. She liked to keep things simple. She believed that God would "supply all her needs according to His purposes," but she was not to ask for "frills."[15]

Those related to the Center knew that it was Edna's faith that built the building. Her friend and supporter Rev. Ralph Beaty, financial officer of the Center who would become Indiana Baptist Convention executive secretary in 1967, attempted to describe Edna's trust: "I call it blind faith. She believed without a doubt that God is able to do anything."[16] Others, like Lynn, Judge Harold Fields, and even Mayor Richard Lugar, were drawn to her vision and mission of changing lives in the Martindale community, a neighborhood where too frequently lives were wasted and debased. It was her simple faith that amazed them.

Another example of that mind-boggling faith is demonstrated in a simple story. One day, while she was sitting in her office at the Center, a grief-stricken old man called Edna. His dog, his only companion, recently died. Sad and in despair, the man told her how lonely it was without his longtime friend. They prayed over the telephone, and Edna assured him that all would turn out well. Fifteen minutes later the telephone rang. The voice on the other side asked whether Edna knew someone who needed a dog. Edna replied, "I've been expecting your call."[17]

On another occasion, the children at the Center had nothing to eat. No food was on the shelves or in the storage area. Edna asked staff and children to make a circle and hold hands while she prayed. She offered up her prayer and just as she said

"Amen," Reverend Beaty and other supporters from the First Baptist Church of Franklin drove up with a truckload of food. "I knew someone would come," she declared.

Rev. Orville Sutton laughed when he remembered Edna telling him about the occasion. "'The hot dogs came in the front door and the buns came in the back,' she related, her black eyes dancing."[18]

Staff members frequently told of the elderly woman who lived near the Center who had such faith in Edna's faith that she would call periodically to ask Edna if it was going to rain. She wanted to hang out her wash.[19]

Her faith was an amazement to those who knew her. Beaty recalled one layman who had witnessed one of Edna's miracles of blind faith. "Here I am," this person said of his reaction to Edna's faith, "this sophisticated, white, waspy person you see. Now I think faith is great. I think it is a wonderful thing, but her [Edna's] faith was an 'it's going to happen' faith, a totally accepting faith."[20]

CHAPTER THIRTEEN

Work in the House That Faith Built

When the Caroline Avenue building was dedicated on 20 June 1965, Edna Martin led a litany with these words, "We are gathered in this Holy Place on this day because God has called us together to hallow this building and these grounds. We are met here only because God in His wisdom and love has seen fit to use us and bless us; therefore, our spirit on this occasion is one of thankfulness and praise." The people responded: "We give thanks to thee, O go recount thy wondrous deeds."

Then, in her litany, Edna admonished those present. "We are filled with admiration and appreciation for the outstanding workmanship which is all about us here today, but we are not deceived, for we know from long years of experience, that unless the Living Lord be present, our building is in vain." In the midst of the excitement of that special occasion, with all the honored guests, the inspirational music, and the honors and accolades, Edna wanted to set the record straight.[1]

The work at the Caroline Avenue location thrived. Edna's concerns over troubled young people and troubled families continued to be at the heart of the program. Her care for young men caught up in the court system developed into a prison program in 1968. She visited the Indiana State Reformatory at Pendleton and the Indiana State Prison in Michigan City. Through the East Side Christian Center, the Men's Fellowship Club sponsored the prison ministry program. Harold Webster, a chef who worked with the Center, traveled all over the state "in the interest of inmates."[2]

The Center's prison ministry resulted in many former inmates being released to the Center. Edna explained to a group of ministers that the prisoners had to have a place to go, to live, and work before they could be paroled. Then she told them about Frank Ferguson, a former convict, who worked at the Center as a handyman.

One day Frank was out back burning boxes. A well-dressed black woman got out of a Cadillac and walked up to the door. Edna saw her and asked if she could be of help. The woman said she was looking for Frank Ferguson, who was her husband.

Edna Martin Christian Center Archives

East Side Christian Center, Caroline Avenue building, dedicated 20 June 1965.

Gathering her thoughts, Edna offered Mrs. Ferguson coffee and excused herself. Because she respected Frank's dignity and manhood, Edna told Frank to go home, put on his "Sunday suit," and come back to the Center via the front walk. While he jumped the fence, Edna engaged his wife in conversation. Soon Frank came sauntering up the walk and into the Center. The surprised and overjoyed couple embraced each other, and Edna gave them her office to reacquaint and to reminisce. Martin smiled as she told the pastors, "He's gone now. Lives in Peoria, Illinois. He hadn't seen his wife in fourteen years. He found God here. They're living together and running a good business."[3]

Many men owed their freedom and new life to Edna Martin. While in the hospital in 1972 with a broken hip, Edna received a bouquet from someone whose name she did not recognize. The note inside read: "You don't remember me, but you came down to the court house and set me free."[4]

One "crime" Edna could not tolerate was personal filthi-

Edna Martin Christian Center Archives

Girls' class at the new East Side Christian Center on Caroline Avenue.

ness. Edna believed "cleanliness is next to godliness." Rev. Ralph Beaty "told of being at the Center one day when a young woman came in with three small children. Both mother and offspring were filthy. The woman began to pour out a long tale about coming from Mississippi to Indianapolis and being unable to find work. She then asked if the Center would offer her family financial assistance. Edna's first words to her, following this emotional appeal, were, 'Why do you stink so bad?' She gave the woman soap and towels and told her to return when she smelled like a lady."[5]

"That may have seemed harsh," Beaty said, "but what Edna wanted to see was if the mother was willing to do something to help herself. The woman and the children came back clean and were given help."[6]

Edna was extremely concerned over the plight of girls and women. Because there were girls at Indianapolis Public School No. 38, an elementary school just down the street from the Center, having their second baby, and too many families with ten or twelve children, she started her own version of a Planned Parenthood course.

Edna saw that public assistance could be a bane to her people because it often crippled them; however, she felt welfare was necessary for some. She never turned away mothers on welfare. Edna would say, "The money cannot be stretched four weeks many times, especially when there are ten and eleven and twelve children . . . by the first week, all the money is gone."[7] She could not see children go hungry when "American Baptists filled the storage shelves at the Center full of canned foods and foods that have been in their ice boxes too long." But in the process of sharing the food, she set up programs for the welfare parents to teach them how to conserve and stretch the food and make it go further than it ordinarily would.[8]

Transportation became increasingly important to the work, as the outreach program grew with children's choir trips, ball games, outings, Senior Bible class pickups, and hauling a bus-

Edna Martin Christian Center Archives

Edna's dream bus, presented to the Center by the American Baptist men and women. Standing in front of the new bus are Richard Muterspaugh, Thelma Herrington, Paul Crafton, Jon Carlstrom, and Edna Martin.

load of children to the Center every day. The older vans and cars had worn out. In 1966 Edna's dream of a bus to help in the ministry became a reality when Indiana Baptist men presented her with a forty-six-passenger school bus. A new bus purchased with monies from the Lilly Endowment and other funds replaced the old bus in 1973.

By 1968 the Center had a library, programs on housekeeping, tutoring, sewing and cooking classes, arts and crafts, music and worship, nineteen clubs, nine study classes, and parolee supervision. Four basketball teams were perennial champions in the Woodruff Place Baptist Church league, and baseball, organized boxing, a seniors group, and childcare filled out the program. The remedial reading program operated seven classes five days a week for both school age children and adults, serving a population with an education level nearly three years below the average of the city's population.[9]

Ada Harris, one of the mentors of Edna's childhood, had

Adult Bible Study at East Side Christian Center led by Rev. Willard R. Jewell. Rev. Jewell was on the staff of the Center for many years.

introduced leather making to her male students in Norwood several decades earlier. It was not incidental that Edna introduced a class in leather making to the boys' program. The boys loved it as well as the industrial arts program. The boys built birdhouses, shelves, jewelry boxes, and lamps with tools donated by the young people at Tuxedo Park Baptist Church.

Sometimes people would ask Edna, "Do you teach religion at the Center?" Edna wrote, "To answer such a question we must know what the person asking the question means by religion. If he means some particular creed, some denominational doctrine such as Lutheran, Methodist, Catholic, etc.," then "the answer would be no. If the Christian philosophy is the way of life, the rights of others, the golden rule, the brotherhood of man and the fatherhood of God, then we must plead guilty."[10]

Volunteers, staffers, and board members remembered when Edna would call them at odd hours to come to the Center and

Events, such as this children's operetta, were well received by the community. The summer 1964 *East Side News–Notes* reported that 250 proud parents watched the Center's Pre-School Day Nursery's performance of "Henny Penny."

pick up food or kids when plans would break down.

"The phone would ring at 6 A.M.," Rev. Richard Padrick, who later directed the work at the Center, recalled, "and I would know it was Edna. She would say, 'The bus driver has not shown up. Come now and get the bus and pick up the kids.' You didn't question Edna. You just went." When asked how he felt about that, he replied, "Well, that was just Edna. She thought that my sense of ownership in the Center work should be so strong, I would understand the importance of my being there, regardless of other plans I might have made."[11]

The community would turn out by the droves for Center events—Sunday afternoon vespers, open houses, Mother's Day teas, operettas, and bazaars. The annual assembly, held in local churches, provided an opportunity to bring in successful black role models as speakers. For example, Rev. C. T. H. Watkins, pastor of Bethel AME Church, who then was president of the city park board, spoke at the annual assembly at St. John Missionary Baptist Church in June 1962.¹² R. K. Smith of the Senate Avenue YMCA sponsored father and son banquets.

A trip to the Shrine Circus turned into an adventure aside from seeing the elephants and the clowns. Edna needed a bus driver to take the children to the Indiana State Fairgrounds, so she called Rev. J. D. Williams, who worked with her at the Center. When he arrived, she told him she had to load 105 children on the bus.¹³

"You don't mean that bus, do you, Sister Martin," he asked, looking at the vehicle parked by the Center.

"Yes," she replied. "That bus."

"But it's a forty-six passenger bus," he pleaded.

Ignoring his skeptical presence, Edna set about seating all the children—four and sometimes five per seat.

"One hundred and five on a forty-six passenger bus," Williams uttered, shaking his head with dismay.

Nevertheless, he climbed into the bus, started it up, and proceeded down the highway toward Thirty-eighth Street and the fairgrounds. Every time a police car would drive beside them, his heart would "come up" out of his chest.

Edna told him not to worry; "The Lord is with you." He was not so sure the Lord wanted them to be that foolhardy. They both prayed. "Being a preacher, I thought I 'knew' how to pray," he said, "But she out prayed me."

The adventure over, they made it safely back to the Center— 105 happy and tired children, one frazzled pastor bus driver, and one "I told you not to worry, God will take care of it" Edna Martin.

No matter how busy she was, Edna never failed to hug the kindergartners, inspect the crafts, cheer for the basketball team, taste the food in cooking class, and listen to the remedial readers. A disruptive boy or a tearful little girl would find Edna pulling them into her office where they would sit on her lap for a few minutes in her comfortable rocker and laugh at Trixie, her parakeet, chattering for attention.¹⁴ Soon the rambunctiousness

Nursery children busy at work at the Center.

would turn to calm and the tears to smiles.

Edna had come a long way from that fourteen-dollar-a-month rented room that started with two little sisters on a dirty doorstep and a dream, but she still was looking out for the children.

Edna did not focus her attention only on her work at the new building. She knew that many people would have to join together to make a dent in problems of the Martindale neighborhood. In spite of the new facility, children still played in trash-littered streets with little supervision. Teenagers were caught up in all kinds of trouble, including prostitution, robbery, and numbers running. Houses—windows shattered by vandals' rocks—were posted with signs reading, "Unfit for Human Habitation." Drug operations ran out of many of the homes. Violent crime was on the increase, and the streets were unsafe.

Cutting across the heart of the area, eating up dwellings and businesses as it progressed, crawled Interstate 70—a symbol of progress to the many who lived outside the area, but an object of devastation and division to those who lived in the elevated path of its reinforced-concrete shadow.[15]

CHAPTER FOURTEEN

Winds of Change and Bright, Hip Kids

The 1960s brought whirlwinds of change to the East Side Christian Center along with the rest of the country. The U.S. bombing of North Vietnam and the antiwar demonstrations, the Civil Rights protests, and the assassinations of President John F. Kennedy, Dr. Martin Luther King, Jr., and Robert F. Kennedy were the strongest gales.

Among the changes to the Center was the coming of a group of dedicated and educated young men and women wanting to work with the poor and disadvantaged, breathing new life and energy into the program. A number of those young men were fulfilling requirements for alternative military service. The war they would fight would be the war against poverty and prejudice.

At first Edna Martin was leery about using conscientious objectors in the program, just as she was leery about anything that might be considered controversial to her constituency. After thinking it over she changed her mind, and the board voted to accept alternative military service volunteers. Many of these young pacifists became dear sons to her and made important contributions to Center work.[1]

In fall 1962 the board hired Paul Crafton, a graduate of

Indianapolis Arsenal Technical High School, Indiana Central College (now the University of Indianapolis), and the Divinity School of the University of Chicago, to be director of boys' programs. He was the only applicant for the position of boys' director that Edna was willing to accept. Edna knew Crafton well because he was the son of a local American Baptist minister. Although exposed to the more liberal social ideas of an institution of international excellence—the University of Chicago—Crafton was still a "home-town boy." Edna felt a degree of comfort with Crafton. More important for the future of the Center, he had proven experience in the field of social work.

Not only would he work with Edna at the Center, he and his wife, Sue Breedlove Crafton, would supervise Fellowship House. Many young people who were volunteering with urban projects under the Church of the Brethren Volunteer Services or other volunteer agencies stayed in that residence.

Edna Martin Christian Center Archives

Jon Carlstrom, community outreach director of the East Side Christian Center, and Mark Peters and Eileen Schnee of Brethren Volunteer Service, work in the Center. During the 1960s many young people worked as volunteers at the Center.

Furthermore, Sue had worked at the Center while in high school. Her father also was an Indianapolis Baptist pastor. Sue had won Edna's heart, and Sue loved Edna. She had promised Edna that someday she would return to work at the Center.

Paul had his reasons for accepting the position at the Center. "Like many in the 60s generation, I questioned authority, but my reaction to Edna Martin was that what she did with her authority was reasonable and made sense. Her success came out of her intelligence and depth of spirituality. If it had not been for the authenticity of her faith and intuitiveness, I could not have accepted her authority."[2]

Another positive result of the Crafton hiring was that in order to bring him into the program, the board agreed to raise Edna's salary from $3,400 to $5,000. This overdue action brought Crafton great satisfaction. "Even at that, she was underpaid," he said. "Sue and I felt that it was unfair that more and more was

Edna Martin Christian Center Archives

The staff of the East Side Christian Center. Paul Crafton, program director, stands in the back row next to Edna Martin. Crafton brought a dedicated group of young, white volunteers to the Center.

expected from Edna with regards to her administrative skills at the same time that she was bearing the primary responsibility for fundraising for the new building program. Many of the board shared this view."[3]

Fellowship House, located at 1714 Brookside Avenue, was at the heart of the volunteer work at the Center in the 1960s. It was a project of the Baptist Youth Fellowship and an outgrowth of the Craftons' involvement with the Brethren volunteer services in Chicago. Paul, as a seminary student at the University of Chicago in 1961, interned with the West Side Christian Parish, an inner-city ecumenical corporation supported primarily by community churches in Chicago's suburbs as well as numerous grants.

Prior to Paul's coming to Indianapolis, one of his duties was to supervise Project House at 1746 W. Fifteenth Street in Chicago, a place where volunteers from the Church of the Brethren alternative service program stayed. Many of these young people were heavily involved in the Civil Rights movement, as were the Craftons. "We knew that real change in that setting [West Side Christian Parish, Chicago] had to involve power, political processes, and much more if life on the West Side was to ever change for the better," Paul said.[4]

When the Craftons returned to Indianapolis, they brought with them the concept of Fellowship House. Men and women who had a passion for community service and Christian social action soon found their way to the fellowship project. Some of these young, idealistic kids worked at the Center, some at area churches, some at other centers, and some with school programs. In all, approximately twenty young people through Fellowship House assisted Edna in her work during the critical years of securing a new building. The involvement of Fellowship House made it possible for her to maintain a strong program at the same time that she was expending her energy with the promotion of the building program and the ongoing operation of the Center.[5]

Crafton recalled, "We were not exactly the kind of white

folks the kids of the Center were used to seeing. We were young and kind of hip and into the times, yet we were also Christians. I like to think we were good role models in that we crossed some barriers and opened up some different kinds of dialogue."[6]

Marsha Bridwell McDaniel, minister of education at First Baptist Church of Indianapolis, who lived at Fellowship House and volunteered at Woodruff Place Baptist Church, learned survival skills very quickly from her contacts at the Center. She wrote to her parents in June 1963, "Before the summer is over, I should be a good referee. So far on the [church] parking lot, we've had three fights. I've never seen such cocky boys. Tomorrow I'm going to the Center to observe and learn how I can do better on the lot on Friday."[7]

Marvin Jones, from the Lake Avenue Baptist Church in Rochester, New York, was a full-time volunteer at the Center doing anything from coaching a basketball team to planning crafts for a boys' club and helping at the Sales House. Sue Whitmore from South Whitley, Indiana, one of the many young women who came to live at Fellowship House, joined him and helped with the girls' programs.

Soon another young man came who would leave his special mark on the work of the Center—a young man that Edna would come to love. The Church of the Brethren had first sent Jon Carlstrom to California in the early 1960s to help in the sorting and shipping of materials to missionaries. Carlstrom felt stifled in the warehouse atmosphere and yearned for an opportunity to witness and serve on a more personal basis. The Brethren sent him to Indianapolis and Edna Martin in 1963. Edna looked him over and decided to give him more lessons in humility and servanthood. She put him to work in the "stifling" and uninspiring job of sorting and distributing clothes in the Sales House.

Carlstrom, who married Fellowship House volunteer Janet Coers, told of other lessons he learned from Edna in the eight years of working with her, eventually as her associate director. He had not been around many African Americans before entering the Brethren program, especially women. "She was impressive," he said. Her strength, humility, and commitment continually amazed him.[8]

He remembers particularly a day when he was trying to think of ways to instill pride in his class of boys, and he decided to put up a poster that read "Be Somebody." Edna came into the room, looked at his handiwork and said, "Jon, you take that thing down. Everybody here is somebody."[9] That phrase would later become a part of the logo for the Center: "Edna Martin Christian Center, Where Everybody Is Somebody and Jesus Christ Is Lord."

Rev. Ralph Beaty stressed the effectiveness of the young volunteers of Fellowship House. "We paid those kids only fifteen or twenty dollars a month. Nevertheless, they loved working at the Center." "They said," Beaty recalled, "college isn't anything compared to this." Beaty added, "Of course, Edna Martin trained them. She was a great trainer. And they loved her."[10]

James W. McDaniel was one of the "fifteen or twenty dollars a month kids" who came to the Center in 1967 through Brethren volunteer services. The volunteers received room and board as well as medical services. Vice president and chief financial officer for Baptist Homes of Indiana, McDaniel remembers how Edna taught him humility, a biblical quality she prized highly. Although a college graduate, his duties included floor care, general maintenance, and bus driving, as well as working with the fifth and sixth grade boys in the afternoon program and the junior and senior highs in the evening.

"One of my strongest memories is from the first week I was there. I was helping arrange the main room for a Christmas program. If I suggested that a table should go on the left, Mrs. Martin said, 'No, it goes on the right.' If I said to put chairs in a row, she said, 'No, put them in a circle.' This went on the whole evening. She countered everything I said, greatly demoralizing me. The next day I went into her office to seek an explanation. She said that the night before the room set-up, I had told some of the senior highs what to do in a bossy, non-caring way. They complained to her, asking if they had to take orders 'from this white boy.' So she decided to teach me humility and show the teenagers that I was not the boss. I never had that problem again."[11]

Edna was always the boss. There was no question about that, although this particular incident seems a contradiction to her customary caring nature and humility. Edna could be intimidating. The tactic she used with McDaniel could be so demoralizing that some other young person would not see in it a lesson of Christian humility but of rancor and humiliation. In McDaniel's case, the observation of other traits of her character or performance resulted in him using the experience in a constructive way. McDaniel affirmed, "She ran the show and everyone else was a supporting cast member, even though other teachers led the Christmas programs and other events, her hand was lovingly and definitely there."[12]

Days of Unrest, the Rock, and
Dr. Martin Luther King, Jr.

Jon Carlstrom, director of community outreach at the East
Side Christian Center in the 1960s, the period of civil
unrest and action, saw firsthand Edna Martin's reaction to
the approach used by many in the black community and in
civil rights organizations. When riots swept the nation and
antiwar protest demonstrations became increasingly more
common, she disdained to participate in any militant
activities or publicly support locally planned marches and
demonstrations.[1]

Edna saw the value in what Dr. Martin Luther King, Jr., and
other leaders in the Southern Christian Leadership Conference
(SCLC) were doing, having herself been a victim of racial prejudice. She knew that conditions needed to be better for blacks,
but she did not agree with the SCLC's methods and she did not
feel that its ways were the right ways to change lives. Edna did not
believe in marches or protests. She felt the way to accomplish her
"dream" of changing people's lives was to serve them and love
them in the name of her Lord. When asked to participate in
protests, Edna would quietly say, "I depend on the Lord for
support, not marches!"

"I really think there was much about the [Civil Rights] movement Edna did not understand," Carlstrom said, "but I know she did not oppose it philosophically. I believe she understood the impact of King's ministry."[2] Paul Crafton agreed with Carlstrom, "She felt the real change had to come in people's hearts, and you could not force it."[3]

Edna respected King. They had a number of things in common. He had graduated from an American Baptist Seminary, Crozer, and was an American Baptist pastor. They had the same dream for children. She was concerned though that the marches and protests had veered far away from "the Rock."

Edna was not in Green Lake, Wisconsin, when King spoke to the staff and guests at the American Baptist Assembly in August 1956 and explained his concept of nonviolent resistance.

> Another basic factor in the method of non-violent resistance is that this method does not seek merely to avoid external physical violence, but it seeks to avoid internal violence of spirit. And at the center of the method of non-violence stands the principle of love. Love is always the regulating ideal in the technique and the method of non-violence. And this is the point at which the non-violent resister follows the love and Saviour Jesus Christ. For it is this love ethic that stands at the center of the Christian faith, and this stands as the regulating ideal for any move, for any struggle to change conditions of society.[4]

Maybe if Edna had been there to hear his explanation, she would have understood how close they really were in purpose.

In December 1958 King spoke at Cadle Tabernacle in Indianapolis before four thousand people as part of the Monster Meeting series sponsored by the Senate Avenue YMCA, and he returned the next year for the same event. At the 1958 meeting King said, "Don't go out to be a good Negro Teacher, a good Negro Doctor, or a good Negro skilled laborer. But go out to do your job so well that no one including the living, the dead, and the unborn could do it better."[5] He also cautioned the audience, "We must learn to live together as brothers or we will die as fools."[6]

Edna would certainly have agreed with King's statement, voicing the same sentiment time and time again. She may not have attended these events, even though she and her husband were strong supporters of the Monster Meetings. Dr. Andrew J. Brown, pastor of St. John's Missionary Baptist Church and an Indianapolis civil rights leader, "noted that few clergymen attended the lectures by King because they were afraid of alienating local benefactors by directly associating with nonviolent protesting."[7] Edna may have shared the sentiments of these clergymen.

King preached, along with Ralph Abernathy, in July 1961 to an overflow crowd at Edna's beloved Mount Zion Missionary Baptist Church to support the Indianapolis chapter of the National Association for the Advancement of Colored People (NAACP). Thousands attended the event, and many were turned away.

Paul Crafton, who was not yet on staff with her at the time, doubts that Edna would have gone. Many blacks of her generation did not support the Civil Rights movement. There was still a definite stamp of the philosophy of Booker T. Washington of Tuskegee Institute in the perception and biases of many older blacks. Washington was an accommodationist who felt that blacks would make better progress by adhering to the prejudices and mores of the "better class" of whites.[8] It was not that they felt the injustices of the past did not need correcting, but they felt there was a danger in the direction King and the nonviolent movement was taking. Like Edna, they could not really believe that better conditions for blacks would come about as a result of the marches and protests. The risk was too great.

"We didn't really understand what it [the Civil Rights movement] was all about," Celestine D. Pettrie, Edna's neighbor, also a Center board member, would explain. "Those were dangerous times. You were afraid to be set out and be counted. You could be called a Communist. That was happening. We had to be extra careful. My husband [who was a teacher at Crispus Attucks High School] had served in the army. I really thought that our phone was tapped. You may have felt strongly that there was good reason for the marches and protests, but you were afraid of what might happen."[9]

Mike Ransom, the son of F. B. Ransom, who was Madam C. J. Walker's attorney, recalled those times in an interview with Greg Stone, author of a study of black Indiana. When Ransom returned from graduate school at Harvard University, he became active in the NAACP and the Progressive party. Because of his involvement as state president of the NAACP and as a Progressive, he was subjected to taunts of "Communist." His wife and sister-in-law lost government jobs. "When they fired my wife, the rest of the people were intimidated, you see. And you're not going to find many people who are going to stick their neck out. We had a few labor type people, but most of the black middle class and the upper class were in the Democratic or Republican Party, and they kind of hung back. There were some ministers, [but] they've come on much stronger after King."[10]

Dr. Andrew J. Brown, an officer of the Center board of directors, probably would have appreciated Edna's support for projects such as Operation Breadbasket and other programs of the SCLC. In reality, he probably was not surprised when he did not get it. Brown understood and respected Edna. He understood what she was trying to do. He was always her friend.

"Edna and Andrew were good friends; they loved each other, but they seldom agreed on anything," Rosa Lee Brown, Dr. Brown's widow, recalled with a smile. "The black community was very close knit, and there were several black neighborhoods—Indiana Avenue, the near north side where Edna lived, the Martindale area, for example—and each was a little cloistered

Rev. Andrew J. Brown

area. Folks did not venture much out of their neighborhood. Edna could not see that a Civil Rights movement or anything could bring the black communities in Indianapolis together, let alone blacks and whites or a whole nation."[11] Edna was not the only one to feel that way. Many of the ministers were reluctant to get involved, especially those who worked for white employers. They feared losing their jobs if they were outspoken about civil rights issues. Mrs. Brown remembered, "My husband would get very discouraged about this attitude, although he could understand it."[12]

In an interview with *Indianapolis News* reporter Frank Salzarulo in April 1965, Dr. Brown said many in the black community who had been sponsored by the white community, and who felt they had "obligations to that white community more so than with the Negro community," did not want "to rock the boat."[13] Dr. Brown was frustrated. "People were bad off. I think people were still frightened. It (protest movement) didn't take off like I expected it to. They had been conditioned to believe more in white folks than in themselves."[14]

Almost forty years later, in a roundtable session sponsored by the Polis Center of Indiana University–Purdue University at Indianapolis and its project on the church and urban culture, Dr. Raymond Sommerville, assistant professor of church history at Christian Theological Seminary, commented on the attitudes of members of black churches during the Civil Rights struggle. "There were a lot of black churches who didn't support Martin Luther King—who had to be prodded and cajoled to support the movement. It would be wrong to assume that, even during the civil rights movement, all black ministers and black churches were suddenly prophetic radicals. Many were still accommodationists, or grassroots revivalists."[15]

Edna, according to Robert M. Franklin's typology referred to by Sommerville,[16] would be a combination of a grassroots revivalist and a pragmatic accommodationist. She focused on personal salvation and individual responsibility, yet she wanted to work within the democratic and capitalist systems while seeking ways to expand resources to those not currently benefiting from it. During Edna's day, and even in the present day, most black churches fall into these two categories.[17]

Although she personally would not go, Edna gave Carlstrom permission to participate in the August 1963 "I Have a Dream" march on Washington, D.C., on behalf of the Center.

Even her sponsoring organization, the American Baptist Home Mission Society, urged Edna to become more involved in civil rights issues. The Baptist Society had a Neighborhood Action Program and wanted its Christian centers to take a strong stand on issues of race, housing, and employment. In a letter sent out to supporters, Edna explained her philosophy: "East Side Christian Center does not carry banners, or go on marches—but in life and practice, we demonstrate. . . . We continue to make a positive contribution toward making a reality that God's earth, His power, and His glory be shared by all of His people."[18]

The Line in the Sand, Hidden Tears, and Edna's Manifesto

Most Americans struggled with the diverse issues of the Civil Rights movement in the 1960s, but for Edna Barnes Martin, who was nearing seventy years of age, those times were charged with dangerous winds that could mortally shake loose her beloved house upon the Rock.

Rev. Frank Alexander, pastor of Oasis of Hope Baptist Church, who succeeded Edna Martin as director of the East Side Christian Center after her death, felt that Edna's position on the Civil Rights movement was consistent with her understanding of the basis of the support for her work. He explained that Edna was in the midst of realizing her dream of a new building, funded by the Lilly Foundation and the Baptists of Indiana and Indianapolis. Many, if not most, of the white Indiana Baptist churches would not have approved of any connection to the Civil Rights movement,[1] even though the American Baptist Convention had publicly supported Dr. Martin Luther King, Jr. In fact, King had been one of the main worship leaders at the 1964 American Baptist Convention where the delegates struggled over the issues of the civil rights bill and other issues of race and justice. King received the Edwin T. Dahlberg Peace Award at the convention.[2]

Richard Padrick, a board member who later became Center director, was certain that most of the grassroots people he pastored in Indiana American Baptist churches would not have been pleased if Edna, in any way, appeared to be in agreement with the Southern Christian Leadership Conference (SCLC).[3] Edna was not alone; many white pastors in Indiana churches also had to walk a fine line. Rev. L. Eugene Ton, president of the Center board in the late 1960s and later executive minister, American Baptist Churches of Greater Indianapolis, recalled that preaching or even referring to issues of race in the pulpit during those times was risky.[4]

Although Indiana Baptists may have had reservations about civil rights issues, they had no reservations about Edna. If Edna said she was using their money only to advance the Gospel, that alone was good enough for them.

Paul Crafton recalls that when Edna really needed someone to talk to, she would frequently turn to R. K. Smith, the highly respected executive secretary of the Senate Avenue YMCA, in many ways the heart of the black community. Smith had been her friend for many years, and his mature wisdom and counsel would calm her down.[5]

Other black organizations were trying to avoid any issues that might prove political or controversial. Flanner House was perhaps the most widely recognized black agency in Indianapolis. Flanner House's director Cleo Blackburn "was rarely active in overt political activity, perhaps owing to his sources of support, which came largely from the white community."[6] Blackburn had come to Flanner House in 1935, just a few years before Edna began her work. The Flanner House Board, similar to the Center's board, was composed of both blacks and whites. Flanner House, however, was a larger, more sophisticated program, with a broader base of support, especially from the earlier form of the United Way—the Community Chest.[7]

Edna wanted nothing to do with Community Chest support. She feared that such support would hamper or even eliminate the religious message of the Center, chipping away at the Rock.

In spring 1966 Edna joined forces with Dr. Andrew J. Brown; Dr. F. Benjamin Davis, pastor of New Bethel Missionary Baptist Church; Rev. Bernard Strange of St. Rita Catholic Church; and Rev. Louis Deer of the Broadway Christian Center. They were promoting a joint participation between the Indianapolis Public Housing Authority, Indianapolis Redevelopment Commission, the churches, neighborhood agencies, and people of a five-block area on the east side bounded by Nineteenth and Twenty-first Streets and Sheldon Street and Hillside Avenue, to construct a racially mixed public housing development.[8] Although this project failed, Edna did cooperate many times with other local churches and community leaders to promote improved conditions in the area. She knew that Jon Carlstrom was involved, with her consent, in the Community Action Against Poverty Project, "Home Is Before Highways." It was an effort to have the city replace the value for the property that would be destroyed by the construction of Interstate 70. That project was successful.

Edna did not object when volunteers, such as Crafton and Carlstrom, attended local meetings of the SCLC at Brown's church. Perhaps more important, she never counseled that they make clear they were not there representing the Center.[9] During this time, certain members of the black community such as Snookie Hendricks drew both her rare ire and her sense of humor.

Hendricks, who started the Indianapolis chapter of the Black Radical Action project, was a lightning rod for controversy. The 21 April 1968 *Indianapolis Star* quoted from a speech Hendricks gave to a group of business and civic leaders: "We don't want to riot, to burn, to raise a lot of hell. . . . We are not trying to create turmoil between races, but we don't want to have to keep marching to prove we are the Americans you say we are."[10]

Hendricks was recalled by Indiana state representative William Crawford as an intimidating man "with a prison record

A little girl looks at the riot police during the 27 July 1969 march in Indianapolis led by Rev. Jesse L. Jackson and Dr. Andrew J. Brown. The march was a call for improved housing and employment for blacks.

who dressed and talked different. A man who proudly confronted white society with his African roots."[11] But, Hendricks
did not intimidate Edna Martin. According to Carlstrom, Edna
asked Hendricks, who had a hangout east of the Center, to
come to her office a number of times. Edna wanted him to
know that she did not approve of the more radically militant
activities of the Black Panthers and his Black Radical Action
project. She knew that several young men involved in Center
programs had been influenced by the Black Panthers and
Malcolm X, and she was not happy about that. "Snookie probably got one of Edna's grandmotherly, no nonsense lectures,"
Carlstrom said.[12] Edna was probably one of the few in
Indianapolis who would dare to lecture Hendricks. In Edna's
presence, Hendricks was respectful. Although he may have
considered her an "Uncle Tom," Bible-preaching woman, he
knew she was well regarded in the community and knew better
than to criticize her publicly.

Edna thought she understood Hendricks. She was more
than a bit amused by his pomposity,[13] and, while seldom
uncharitable in her remarks, she found little good to say about
Hendricks. "Edna knew Snookie's character," Celestine Pettrie
recalled, "She felt she knew where his heart was."[14] "Snookie
was foolin' with the wrong person if he went up against
Grandma," grandson James Robert Martin would later say.[15]

An estimated crowd of two thousand, led by Rev. Jesse L.
Jackson, Dr. Andrew J. Brown, and Indiana state representative
David L. Allison, gathered 27 July 1969 at St. John's Missionary
Baptist Church and marched about five miles to the governor's
mansion. The purpose of the march was to plead for improved
housing and employment for Indianapolis blacks.[16] Edna did
not participate.

"She never engaged in rhetoric. Never went on a march. What
she did changed more lives than all the protests could have done
in her neighborhood, as she defined it," Carlstrom recalled.[17]

The night King was shot, 4 April 1968, Sen. Robert F.

Kennedy was speaking at a gathering at a near north side park in Indianapolis. James McDaniel remembers vividly what happened that night.

> We had taken a bus load of kids from the Center to the park to hear Kennedy speak. He arrived late, and as he stood up to speak, Kennedy asked others on the platform with him, "Have they been told yet?"and heads indicated "no." Then Kennedy turned to the crowd gathered around and told them, "Dr. Martin Luther King has been shot and killed." There were outcries of disbelief and sorrow. I looked around the mainly black crowd, and I began to be concerned for my safety and the safety of the other whites with us from the Center. We began to gather the kids up and head them quickly toward the bus back to the Center. [18]

Carlstrom recalled, "I was there at Seventeenth and Broadway, and I heard Kennedy speak the words [that King had been killed]. My heart stopped. I had chills. I wondered what would happen next."[19]

There was concern throughout the Indianapolis community that night. Many felt the calming words of Kennedy, and the promises made by Mayor Richard Lugar the next day kept trouble from occurring. Crafton remembers there was also great consternation at the Center. "I remember seeing Edna in her office crying, but on outward appearances, she soon regained her composure. She did not want to appear to be weak and lacking in trust in God's purposes. She was her own person. There was always a piece of Edna that was hers alone."[20]

Ironically, in spite of Edna's stand against militancy, the militant movement did seriously affect the Center's stability, especially in the late 1960s with James Forman and "The Black Manifesto." When Forman, director of United Black Appeal, read "The Black Manifesto" at the National Black Economic Development Conference in Detroit, Michigan, on 26 April

Bass Photo Company Collection #C5490, Indiana Historical Society

A busload of kids from the Center was in the audience on the night of 4 April 1968. Here, Robert F. Kennedy is announcing the sad news of the assassination of Dr. Martin Luther King, Jr.

1969, and later from the pulpit of Riverside Church, New York City, a pulpit vacated by the church's ministers,[21] there was a great outcry from the white religious community.

The manifesto called for reparations of $500 million from white churches and Jewish synagogues as payment for slavery, in addition to many other demands. Forman made it clear in the manifesto that force was a viable option if the demands were not met. "We are not threatening the churches. We are saying that we know the churches came with the military might of the colonizers and have been sustained by the military might of the colonizers. Hence, if the churches in colonial territories were established by military might, we know deep within our hearts that we must be prepared to use force to get our demands."[22]

Many leaders and organizations in the black community joined in support of the manifesto, including some of the more moderate groups, such as the National Committee of Black Churchmen. Most major denominations rejected the manifesto but felt compelled to address the wrongs that had been committed against African Americans. Dr. Dallas West, executive secretary of the Indiana Baptist Convention, stated the position of the executive committee of the Indiana Baptist Convention in an article in *The Baptist Observer*: "Though we reject the philosophy of the Manifesto and the tactics used to implement it, this in no way suggests that we are opposed to the obvious and legitimate needs of black people. We urge the ministry of the American Baptist Convention to the black people of America be continued and enlarged through our regular channels."[23]

West stated that according to the *New York Times*, "If James Forman and his followers attempted to occupy the denomination's headquarters at Valley Forge, Pennsylvania, Dr. Thomas Kilgore, the first black president of the American Baptist Convention, said 'we would try to carry on business as usual. But, if violence erupted, we would have them removed forcibly. There comes a time when one must resort to constituted authority.'"[24]

By the end of the 1960s, rumor and gossip circulated in

some of the white Baptist churches throughout the state that the Center was a meeting place for "militant" blacks supporting "The Black Manifesto." Monetary contributions for the Center from white churches substantially decreased, and the Center suddenly had a twenty-five-thousand-dollar deficit.

The demarcations between Edna's three worlds were drawn again, and she had to make her stand clear. She was quick to communicate to her white supporters, "I reject demands from any as are included in the 'Black Manifesto,'" and she reminded them that she had served them faithfully for nearly thirty years. She avowed, "East Side Christian Center programs are planned for the healing of the whole individual. We solicit your continued prayers and financial support as we here, Black and White together, strive to make whole our society as God intended it to be."[25]

Rev. Ralph Beaty, executive minister of the Indianapolis Baptist Association, came to Edna's defense with this letter to churches.

> East Side Christian Center is committed to Jesus Christ. The building was built and the program established for that purpose alone. Therefore, the Center cannot and should not be identified with the demands of the Black Manifesto in any way. Whereas many of the supporters of the Black Manifesto want to overthrow the government, our present economic system and destroy the church, the East Side Christian Center seeks to win people to Christ, teach the truths found in the scriptures and enrich the lives of people.[26]

Indiana Baptists responded in love to Edna's stand, establishing a new high for donations to the Center. In 1969 contributions were $22,859.03, with 189 American Baptist churches and 19 churches of other denominations contributing to the ongoing work of the Center.[27]

Rev. L . Eugene Ton, president of the board, wrote in *News N' Notes* from the Center in February 1969:

Each year brings new challenges to any institution, but it seems that in these days of such social and economic revolution, it is more true than it has ever been before. Nineteen sixty-nine promises to be an eventful year for East Side. Some of the events we can anticipate, such as taking possession and establishing a meaningful Christian program in the newly purchased building on Roosevelt Drive [the Youth Center and Sales House]. Other events we cannot anticipate, as only the force of time and the chemistry of man can produce. In each case, East Side Christian Center stands ready to serve and to be a part of the East Side Community.[28]

In the face of criticism from activist leaders of the black community, displeasure from her supporting denomination because she did not take a stronger stand for the Civil Rights movement, and cautious support from her base of financial support, most of which were afraid she would take a stronger stand in the Civil Rights movement, Edna stood firm. Her "Manifesto" was the Rock, which she could defend without reservation, and "all other ground, to her, was sinking sand."

CHAPTER SEVENTEEN

Family Shelter in the Time of Storm

Edna Martin always referred to herself as Mrs. Earl Martin. She loved her husband very much, and to those who knew them, they were devoted to each other and a complement to each other. Earl Martin died just two months before they would have celebrated their golden anniversary.

"My husband has been the man behind the scenes through it all," she told a reporter for the *Indianapolis Times* in 1954.[1] A retired mail carrier, Earl was the man behind the woman in public, but at home things were different. When Edna came home to her neat little house on quiet, middle-class Indianapolis Avenue, she left the world of the Center behind her. According to family and friends, the problems of the day were usually not discussed with her husband. However, if Earl found out someone was giving Edna a hard time, he would say exactly what he thought in no gentle terms. Edna would just look at him and shake her head and say, "Now Earl."

After their daughter Doris Lillian died, Earl Jr. became the focus of their family life. He would become an Indianapolis police officer and reach the rank of sergeant before his retirement, receiving many awards for his duty. Earl Jr. was his

The Martin family: Earl Martin, Edna, and Earl Martin, Jr.

mother's protector. An ace detective, he was aware of the problems and dangers in the community—the drug busts, the vice, the violence. He was concerned for her welfare. He knew that because of her complete faith and trust in God, she would venture into situations that would be dangerous for her.[2]

Married twice, Earl Jr. had four sons and two daughters that were their grandmother's delight. The children spent much time at the Center when they were little and loved to visit their grandparents' home. While Edna would watch Red Skelton on television with the children or fix them little snacks, Earl Sr. would retreat to his basement or out to the little shop he had made in his garage near a pond. There he could skin squirrels and rabbits, work with his fishing tackle, and make projects with his woodworking tools. He had a great electric train set, running all around the basement, that the grandsons could look at but not touch. Everyone in the family knew that Earl Sr. would have a drink and a smoke out in his shop after dinner. Nobody talked about it, and Edna never discussed it.

James Robert Martin, Earl's youngest grandson, grew up with his grandfather's love for hunting and fishing. "I was his bird dog," James remembered. "I would go out and pick up the rabbits."[3] As to whether Edna enjoyed Earl's outdoor hobbies, the answer was simple. Grandson Darrell Richard Martin recalled his grandmother saying one time that she wanted nothing to do with grandpa's huntin', squirrel skinnin', and fishin'. "She said that she was [a] two strings of pearls in a hat lady, not a fishing lady sitting on the bank."[4]

Edna may not have wanted to be a "lady sitting on the bank," but she did enjoy many summers sitting on the porch of a rented cabin at Monterey, Indiana, a short distance from Lake Maxinkuckee and its exclusive resort town of Culver. She would take the grandchildren on boat rides on the lake. Granddaughter Brenda Martin Wilcox remembers that her grandmother did not like the discomforts of outdoor excursions into insect-infested areas though. "One day we were out look-

Courtesy of Martin Family

Edna Martin with grandchildren Alice, James Robert, and Darcia Jo (Brenda) on Lake Maxinkuckee. The Martin family rented a cabin at Monterey, Indiana, for many summers, and Edna enjoyed taking her grandchildren on boat rides on the lake.

ing for Granddad and a couple of the boys, and we stopped the car in an area that was swarming with mosquitoes. Grandma started to open the car door and get out. We yelled, 'Grandma, don't open the door.' But she did, and the mosquitoes descended on her. She started crying out, 'Oh my, Oh my, Oh my,' and flappin' her hands and jumping around. We couldn't help but laugh at her, and she wasn't very pleased with us."[5]

Darrell remembered the many times his grandmother would pick up him and his brother and take them to the Center. They loved to play on the swings, but they could not play until they helped their grandmother move foodstuffs and do other small jobs. "'Do this and do that,' grandmother was always saying." She was always either going to or coming home from the Center, and she expected them to be helpful and busy. According to Darrell, when his grandfather was not at work delivering the mail he was at home messing around with his hobbies, making kites for the kids, and shooting off fireworks for the whole neighborhood.[6]

James Robert Martin especially was impressed with how the toughs and gang members in the neighborhood treated his grandmother. "With respect . . . I mean the street trash, when they hit the Center, and everybody did sooner or later, because . . . the park was wrecked, when they hit the Center, it was 'Mrs. Martin' . . . they could be fighting and she would walk out there and it would be, 'O.K., Mrs. Martin.' . . . She could handle people with a smile and get them to do what she wanted them to do."[7]

She was not always so gentle with her grandchildren. She wanted them to behave. "When I had done something bad," Brenda said, "and she knew about it, Grandma would warn, 'Now I am going to give you time to get yourself together. I expect you to do the right thing. If you can't get yourself together, then I am going to tell your father.'" Brenda sure did not want to hear that. She would plead, "Oh man, no, Grandma. Don't tell Dad." Edna's lessons have served Brenda well over the years. She cherishes Edna's Bible and a Harbrace handbook of English that Edna gave her. Both books have provided her with positive lessons for life.[8]

Edna loved her husband, her son, and her grandsons; but men, in general, did not always fare well in her opinion. She would say to Brenda, mostly in jest, "Men are all snakes. It's in the Bible. Never listen to a man."[9] Brenda laughed when she recalled

Edna with grandson Larry Martin.

her grandmother's sage advice. "I still try and remember that."[10]

To her grandchildren, Edna was just a grandmother who could be fun and could be firm. It would not be until they attended an event where she was honored and praised for her work that they realized her value to the community. Darrell Richard Martin recalled, "I realized she wasn't just a grand-mother anymore . . . she was somebody special."[11]

CHAPTER EIGHTEEN

Earthly Awards, Heavenly Rewards

Edna Martin was never included in a volume of *Who's Who among African Americans*, nor was she selected to appear in the two-volume encyclopedia, *Black Women in America* (1994). Neither was she mentioned in the two-volume collection of *Notable Black American Women* (1992). Only two women from Indiana were selected in *Notable Black American Women* beside Madam C. J. Walker, who was not from Indiana, although her hair products and beauty company brought wealth, fame, and good works to Indianapolis.

Willa Brown (1906–1992), pioneering aviator, activist, and educator, who lived only a short time in the city,[1] was included, as was Patricia A. Russell-McCloud. Born in Indianapolis in 1946, Russell-McCloud graduated from Shortridge High School, completed a distinguished college career, and returned to Indianapolis to teach at Arsenal Technical High School. After receiving a law degree from Howard University, Russell-McCloud left Indiana for Washington, D.C., distinguishing herself again as a Federal Communications Commission attorney. A nationally known motivational speaker, Russell-McCloud frequently encouraged women in her audiences, "Whatever you want to be or do, it's

Edna had always dreamed of visiting places mentioned in the Scriptures. In 1972 friends contributed to funds to make a trip to the Holy Land possible.

your life, and you have a mandate to live it." She stressed, "Good intentions do not make a success. You must move past neutral. You have to get in gear. Step out. Climb up. Get started. Go forth!"[2] She could be describing Edna Martin.

Edna was listed in the National Council of Negro Women Indianapolis Section of *When the Truth Is Told: A History of Black Women's Culture and Community in Indiana, 1875–1950*, by Darlene Clark Hine, published in 1981.[3]

In a speech to the *Indianapolis Recorder* Women's Charities on 5 May 1984, Hine said, "The invisibility and silence surrounding blacks as a whole is lamentable but that surrounding the black woman is doubly oppressive. The black woman, because she is a member of two subordinate groups in this country—women and blacks—is rarely examined in her own terms as a distinct and separate entity. No accurate social history of Indiana, or for that matter, America can be written or taught as long as black women are not included."[4]

Then again, awards or public recognition never impressed Edna. One day a visitor asked to see a recent plaque she had received. She had to think for a moment, and then she had to dig it out from behind a stack of books on the top shelf of her bookcase.[5] It was not that she did not appreciate the recognition she received. It was just that she was more gratified by "the souls saved" at the Center, and the fourteen ministers, many deacons and Sunday school teachers, hundreds of church members, and thousands of good and useful citizens who "as children" had come under her care. "Give credit where credit is due," was Edna's response to those who would heap honors upon her head. "To God Be the Glory!"

In 1956 a number of honors came her way. The Business and Professional Women's committee of the Woman's Committee of the Woman's Convention Auxiliary of the National Baptist Convention, Inc., gave her an award for "outstanding contributions to the religious and civic welfare of the people." Tau Gamma Delta Sorority, Gamma Chapter presented her with an award, "In recognition of [her] ability and achievement as one of the outstanding women of the city." Then the Indianapolis chapter of the National Council of Negro Women honored her in November for her achievements through outstanding service rendered to the public. "Your kindly disposition, patience and forbearance have been an inspiration to all."[6]

In 1962 Edna was the special speaker for Women's Day at the famed Riverside Church in New York City. The speech she gave on that occasion is included in the appendix.

One activist organization to which Edna belonged and which was dear to her heart was the Independent Order of Saint Luke, a mutual-benefit society organized in Richmond, Virginia. The order stood as a model for what local organizing could accomplish. Under the leadership of Maggie Lena Walker, the order adopted an agenda aimed at improving economic opportunities for black women and eliminating segregation and disfranchise-

Edna Martin Christian Center Archives

One honor that was special to Edna Martin was the honorary Doctorate of Humane Letters conferred on her by Franklin College on 6 June 1965. From that time on, she preferred to be called Dr. Edna Martin. Edna is shown with Earl Sr. on the right and Earl Jr. on the left.

ment.[7] Walker, like Edna, was the daughter of a washerwoman, and washerwomen were among its important supporters.

On 6 June 1965, a day that even Edna was willing to admit was very special, Franklin College granted her a Doctorate of Humane Letters. It was in Franklin that she had stood outside in the rain because of the color of her skin and had been served food in a cafeteria only because of the outcry of white women. The award gave credence to the words she had shared with women in other places and other towns, "There will be another day and sooner or later the Spirit will win." She was humbled and deeply touched by the Franklin College tribute. Theretofore, she desired to be referred to as Dr. Edna Martin.

Other awards include a Sertoma International award given by the downtown Indianapolis club in recognition of her outstanding work in the fields of poverty, overcrowded housing, and delinquency. Edna and her assistant and niece Delores

American Baptist Assembly, Green Lake, Wisconsin, Archives

Edna, standing in the far right group of participants, returned to the American Baptist Assembly at Green Lake, Wisconsin, on 13 August 1967 for the dedication of the World Mission Center. This was the scene of her first inspiring Missions Conference in 1946.

At the 36th Annual Summer Conference of American Baptist Women of Indiana, held at Franklin College in June 1972, Edna was surprised with a program in her honor, "This Is Your Life, Dr. Edna Martin."

Mitchell, who had served her for eighteen years in the Center work, were registered at the Essex House for one night as guests of the Sertoma Club. They enjoyed the special treatment.

Edna also received an award from the American Baptist Home Mission Society, in recognition of her outstanding devotion and contributions to the work of the Center. During her tenure as a missionary for the society, she would be honored as one of the few ever commissioned without a formal education, tested as to whether she and her work were worthy of the society's standards, and praised for her Christian witness in the face of extreme obstacles.

On a beautiful summer day, 13 August 1967, Edna returned to the American Baptist Assembly at Green Lake, Wisconsin, to help dedicate the World Mission Center on behalf of all American Baptist missionaries. It was an honor that gave her great joy. She stood, a bit stooped, with other dignitaries beside the stone, wood, and fiberglass structure that would serve as a center for American Baptist mission work. Her thoughts no doubt returned to her first visit to Green Lake in 1946 as representative of the Center at a missionary conference. She could never forget the pageantry of that occasion, the quiet procession to the lakefront where Judson Tower's cross reflected in the rippled water and danced off faces representing missions from all over the globe. Edna thought then that there could never be another event that would mean so much to her—the impoverished little girl who once dreamed of being a missionary to Africa.

Now they called her Dr. Edna Martin. She had been singled out of many that served on mission fields to be a part of this ceremony. Her heart was full of gratitude. The verse, Ecclesiastes 5:4, had kept her on course through all these years, "When you vow to God, do not delay paying it; for he has no pleasure in fools." She had tried to be faithful to her vow.

In April 1971 the Indianapolis Church Federation, which had shown great support and interest in her work since her early days in her first house, recognized Edna for "selfless and devoted Christian service" to the Indianapolis community.[8] The 1941 report of the Church Federation had launched Edna on her children's crusade.

After her death, she was included in the Black Women's History project of the National Council of Negro Women. Her biography is housed with the collection in the National Archives and Research Center in Washington, D.C., the former residence of Mary McLeod Bethune, founder of the council.[9]

One of the highest honors a citizen of Indiana can receive is to be inducted into the Indiana Academy, a project of the Associated Colleges of Indiana, which recognizes distinguished persons who spent an important part of their life in the state. Edna was chosen in 1972 for this honor, in a class of eighteen, which included Eugene S. Pulliam, newspaper publisher; Izler Solomon, conductor of the Indianapolis Symphony Orchestra; Richard G. Lugar, mayor of the city of Indianapolis; and Eli Lilly, chairman of the Board of Eli Lilly and Company and president of Lilly Endowment Incorporated.[10]

One of Edna's highest honors was her induction into the Indiana Academy. Edna shows some of the children at the Center the medallion she received from the Associated Colleges of Indiana.

She was the only woman and the only black. She was the only one without a college education. To Edna, the little girl who once delivered laundry to the stately back door of a Lilly home on Pennsylvania Street, the honor no doubt was doubly significant.

According to some, Edna "had arrived." But Edna would tell you in the words of the Fortieth Psalm that she "arrived" the day, "He set my feet upon a rock making my footsteps firm, And He put a new song in my mouth, song of praise to our God."

All Edna ever wanted for her efforts though was

> To find the lost,
> To heal the broken,
> To feed the hungry,
> To release the prisoner,
> To rebuild the nations,
> To bring peace among brothers,
> To make music in the heart.[11]

CHAPTER NINETEEN

Last Days and the Thief in the Night

Edna Martin may have lied about her age. Many articles and records indicate that she said she was born in 1900, but according to her birth certificate and census records she was born in 1897. She probably cut those three years off her life so she could serve the Lord longer. She had so many children to find and so little time. She could not rest as long as there was one child to be told the story of the brother who rose above slavery to a position of prominence in a land not his own.

The 1970s found Edna weakened by cancer and its treatment but resolute in her desire to see the East Side Christian Center work grow. One of the most important projects to impact the Center's neighborhood in the 1970s was the Soul Ark on Roosevelt Avenue. With a Lilly Endowment grant of $80,000 the Center purchased a warehouse and began operation of a safe haven for teenage boys. Vincente League and Jon Carlstrom of the Center staff developed and conducted the program with more than 125 young people registered.

Many of the young men from the Soul Ark were involved in the basketball program held in the gym at Woodruff Place

Baptist Church. Center teams were always in contention for division trophies, playing teams from other Baptist churches and boys' clubs from as far away as Rushville and Shelbyville. Any young person who disobeyed the rules at the Soul Ark not only met up with the disapproval of League and Carlstrom but also Edna's discipline. It was a different kind of discipline than the boys were accustomed to; it was a discipline driven by love.

"I have great faith in young people," Edna would say. "They are sincere. They have seen hypocrisy in high places. They have been duped. They want the real thing. That is what they are searching for—and this is it!"[1]

When a boy who had become involved in the Soul Ark and who attended regularly was absent one day, Edna went looking for him. There were certain enterprising men in the neighborhood that established businesses including pea-shake houses, and Edna knew they engaged children in their scams. She found the young man in a hole-in-the-wall where all kinds of

Edna Martin Christian Center Archives

The Youth Center, Soul Ark, on Roosevelt Avenue, was made possible by a grant from the Lilly Endowment. It opened with 125 young people registered on 15 November 1970.

vice was occurring. When she went to the door, the lookout shouted for everyone to stop what he was doing because "there's a lady here." She marched into the house and brought the boy out. Later, Edna shared, "I shivered thinking about what could have happened."[2]

In addition to the programs at the Soul Ark, the board adopted a record budget of $78,504 for 1970. Of this, $56,251 was to pay the salaries of the sixteen staff members and the additional $22,253 "would provide program materials, utilities, and the other required costs to operate the center" and its out-posts.[3] A plea went out from the board in March 1970 for help in manning the Sales House—"sorting, pricing and preparing for display the many items we offer for sale." Edna reminded donors just to bring usable items. She softly chided, "We know you will understand that for us to share materials needing repairs with people who cannot repair them would not be a very effective Christian witness."[4]

Edna Martin Christian Center Archives

Many of the young men from the Soul Ark took part in the basketball program at Woodruff Place Baptist Church. The Center teams won many division trophies throughout the years.

Edna wrote about a Christmas in which the Center aided fifty-eight families. "A mother with an ill husband and six children from 2–15 years old, expresses deep gratitude for the food, fuel and clothing we supplied to make their one room home a more cheerful place." She stated that "prayers of thanks and gratefulness were received for a family of 13. The parents and 11 children, the youngest being a 14 month old boy. To them we gave fuel, bedding, food and clothing."[5]

Many of the 1,001 children who attended one of the Christmas parties at the Center received the only Christmas they had. The following is a note from Tony, a ten-year-old boy:

> Dear Mrs. Martin:
>   Tank [sic] you for the party and for the presents. I am grayful [sic] for everything. I would like to show how grayful I am but I can't. Next time I get 5¢, 10¢, or 30¢ I will give to you.
>   Tony [6]

Although she was deathly ill, Edna was adamant in her efforts to continue her work at the Center. She was determined not to die in the first place. She had too much yet to do. She refused to notify the ministers and missionary board of the American Baptist Convention of her illness, afraid that they would not let her continue her work.

"She would come into the office sometimes after her chemotherapy session for her breast cancer, and you could see the redness above the neckline of her dress, but she would never talk about it. She would never mention it, and we would not mention it," Jon Carlstrom said of the time before he left the Center in 1970. "She was so afraid they would make her stop working."[7]

Her friend and board member Rev. Ralph Beaty said, "I had already assured her when she tearfully told me that the Home Missionary Society wanted her to retire after her sixty-fifth birthday, that she was Edna Martin, and she was the founder of the East Side Christian Center. She would retire when she wanted to

Baptist Crusader/Indiana Baptist News Section, *January 1970*

Edna Martin and Rev. Ralph Beaty, executive secretary of the Indiana Baptist Association, at the announcement of Edna's thirtieth year of service with the East Side Christian Center. Beaty said that at seventy, Edna "will continue to be the director [of the Center] until she decides to retire."

retire and not until then. When she made that decision, then we would all rejoice with her."[8]

In 1974 Edna was still working at the Center, serving as director even though she had suffered through radical surgery and the effects of breast cancer, including surgery on her vocal cords. Officially she was no longer under appointment as a missionary of the American Baptist Home Mission Society because of a mandatory age requirement of seventy. In February, after the Center had helped six hundred people to have a better Christmas, she was sending a plea through church newsletters for donations of food, toys, clothing, and fuel for eighty-six families. "People in our area are cold and hungry, and so it looks like we will be helping those in need all winter."[9]

Soon Edna could no longer manage to come to her beloved house on Caroline Avenue, but she was still managing her own life and her own death. Edna would do things her way, even when it came to writing her own funeral service. "She had me pick out what she would wear. She even had me pick out what I would wear," her granddaughter Brenda Martin Wilcox said. "She said, 'I want that front row [of grandchildren] to be in bright colors. Be happy for me.'"[10]

Reverend Beaty also recalled her determination: "When I went to see her just a few days before she died of breast cancer on May 25, 1974, she pretended to eat her dinner so I would think she was well enough to come back to the Center." Beaty continued, "When I left the house, her sister told me, 'she will just throw that dinner up, but she wanted you to think she was getting better.' She was something else. I'll never forget her. Most people that ever knew her would never forget her."[11]

"She was so determined to succeed in her mission. She was so inspiring. She just made everyone want to reach higher," Celestine Pettrie recalled.[12]

Brenda, then a high school senior, stayed with Edna during her last days, bathing, preparing meals, and giving shots to her grandmother. "Grandmother loved flowers. She had them all around the house—peonies and petunias and honeysuckle and roses. When she could no longer go to the Center, she would sit out on the patio and tell me, 'God is here I can feel him here among my flowers.'"[13] Outside the living room window of Brenda's north side condominium, right where she can see them and gain strength from them, are peonies she has transplanted from Edna's yard.

Edna had special words for her only surviving child. To her son Earl Jr., she wrote shortly before her death:

> Death is not an easy thing for anyone to understand, but every life shall one day end—but remember only the body can be taken, and I will still be. Time and accident, illness and weariness may take my body—but remember nothing good ever ends.
>
> Everything alive is a part of each of us—the sun, the earth, the skies, the rivers, the ocean are all a part of each of us.

Take care of your body, and do not abuse it—Be strong spiritually and active. There is nothing you can't do, if you make up your mind to do it, and it is right.

Sometimes the cost of fulfilling a dream is high—be sure it is worth it.

Learn to stand on your own feet and make right decisions—it's your life.

Disappointments and trouble only make you stronger if you trust God, but to be a mountain climber—you have to climb some mountains in your life. "First to thine own self be true, and it must follow as the night, the day—thou cannot be false to any man."

Be good to your family. Be Patient—when they make mistakes, try to understand. Son, I am proud of you—you deserve all that I have done for you and your family.

Do your best—Pray—God will never fail you. You will never be alone.

Mother [14]

Earl Jr. loved his mother dearly. He knew, as she said, that he would never be alone. Earl Jr. passed away 24 February 1988, fourteen years after his mother's death.

Several members of Edna's family tell of an incident that occurred the evening before she died. They were sitting in Edna's home while she lay in her bedroom nearby near death. They heard her call, "Earl, Earl, I'm coming." Then they heard steps—seven steps—just the number it would take to walk from an adjoining bedroom to Edna's. "I was scared to death," Brenda said. "I was afraid to go into Grandma's room. I went to call my mom, and she said, 'Don't be afraid. Just go in and see her. I'll be right there.'" When the grandchildren went to check, Edna was in a coma and was no longer able to speak. "Grandma always said that death would come like a thief in the night, and he did," Brenda said.[15] Edna passed away 25 May 1974.

Crowds came to Edna's funeral; many could not get inside for the service. Leaders of the white and black community spoke, as

The Indiana Baptist Observer, *May 1970*
Mount Zion Missionary Baptist Church, Thirty-fifth Street and Graceland Avenue, the site of Edna's funeral.

did John Lynn, former manager of the Lilly Foundation. As Reverend Beaty was eulogizing Edna, there were the unexpected loud claps of thunder and flash of lightning bolts. Beaty at the podium paused, listening to the sudden fury, and commented that heaven's gates were opening for Edna.[16] There would not be anyone present who would question that conclusion.

CHAPTER TWENTY

Sister of the Solid Rock

Dr. Dadashinarehema (Jeanette) Jones, pastor of an Indianapolis-based African-American church, was once a little "untouchable" three year old who toddled from a tiny row house on Arsenal alley into the door of the East Side Christian Center. "I think her work [Edna Martin's] was on the order of Gandhi." When Jones first came to the Center, she already had experienced rejection from some in her community. "I used to wonder," she mused, "if we were like the untouchables, that caste in India which was below everything and everyone else. I mean, the other people in our neighborhood didn't accept us. I used to wonder why we weren't accepted among our own."[1]

When Jones was a child in Indianapolis, many in the black community had been born in the city and had benefited from schooling and some advances in integration. Children coming up from the South, such as Jones, were more likely to be treated as outsiders. Edna never treated her as an outsider; she drew her into her circle of love.

Jones will never forget those moments seated in a little chair in a circle around Edna, listening to her tell them about

God's word. "She would quietly tell us the scripture for that day. Then she would take her Bible and hold it up before us. She would say, 'Let us concentrate on God's Word. If we keep our minds on Him he will open the Bible to where He wants us to read,'" Jones recalled. "We believed her with all our might. You know, our Bibles would fall open just where she said they would." Jones added with a smile, "When I do what Mrs. Martin told me to do, that still happens to me today."[2]

Jones has received several degrees and has traveled the world as an army nurse, reaching the rank of major in Preventive Health Services. Her ministry is as a physical and spiritual healer, but the measure she sets her standard by is her beloved mentor and "elder," Edna Martin.

Dr. Dallas West, executive minister of the Indiana Baptist Convention from 1956 to 1985, wrote in tribute what Edna meant to him:

> When Dr. Martin poured out her story, people became more human and the gospel more understandable, and people held Edna Martin in their hearts and followed her with their prayers. . . . She not only served East Side Center but served all of us. She taught us to face adversity with courage, to develop energy and enthusiasm when we are tired, to achieve victory in the face of defeat, to have faith in the midst of sorrow. She taught us to understand better what the Apostle Paul meant when he said, "Who shall separate us from the love of Christ? Shall tribulation, or distress, or persecution, or famine, or peril, or nakedness, or sword? No, in all of these we are more than conquerors through Him who loved us."[3]

Rev. Frank Alexander summed up Edna's unique contribution. "Her faith was amazing, and equally amazing was the fact that she did so much with so little. She really proved that a person can take whatever talents and resources that they have and serve God in amazing ways." Alexander pondered whether

Edna's methods would be as effective today. "She understood the times. The times shaped her, but she used the times. When she started her work in the east side, the time was just right for her methods. The methods of a Dr. Andrew J. Brown might not have worked in the 1940s. Perhaps by the 1960s, Edna's methods were not as well suited for the new times. But God lifted her up for such a time."[4]

In 1941 when Edna Martin set her first house upon the Rock in that tiny room, another black woman was making her mark as a pioneer in the education and reformation of black children. Her name was Mary McLeod Bethune. Born twenty years before Edna, of parents who were slaves, Bethune had wanted to be a missionary to Africa. After she worked hard to graduate, Moody Bible Institute told her that the missionary board would not send a black to Africa.[5] Heartbroken, she set her mind to save the children of the South—from the Carolinas

Edna Martin Christian Center Archives

Edna with the children she loved.

to Florida. Bethune started in threadbare quarters with $1.50 seed money, and she took a town dump and made it into what would become Bethune-Cookman College. As Edna would do after her, she interested wealthy, white friends such as John D. Rockefeller, Sr., and James N. Gamble, of the Procter and Gamble Corporation of Cincinnati, Ohio.

Unlike Edna, who did not aspire to a national pulpit for her views, Bethune became president of the National Association of Colored Women and National Council of Negro Women, and director of the National Youth Administration's Division of Negro Affairs.

In 1941, about the time that Edna began her ministry with children, Bethune wrote, "For I am my mother's daughter, and the drums of Africa still beat in my heart. They will not let me rest while there is a single Negro boy or girl without a chance to prove his worth."[6]

Edna Mae Barnes Martin and Mary McLeod Bethune were sisters of the solid rock. Edna's ministry with children was carried out on the streets of the east side of Indianapolis. In the midst of the winds of poverty and oppression and the storms of protests and opposition, Edna would not stray from the Rock of the Gospel of Jesus Christ. She could not rest while there was a single black boy or girl without a chance to prove his or her worth.

The Legacy of Edna Martin

The scene has not changed much outside the Edna Martin Christian Center on Caroline Avenue from the first week it opened its doors in 1964. Standing in front of the yellow cement stone building, one can look up and see the slash of Interstate 70 that took away the lifeblood of homes and businesses in the Martindale community. One can hear the sound of semis roaring toward Columbus, Pittsburgh, or St. Louis. Across from the Center is a scrawny patch of green park littered with whiskey bottles and paper trash. Just a block away over the tops of homes is the brick skeleton of Indianapolis Public School No. 38—a graveyard of neighborhood hopes and dreams.

Just as Larry Rood's study of 1962 described, there are still many residents without high school diplomas, on welfare rolls, without employment, and in substandard houses. It is still a high-crime area—drive-by shootings, murders, rapes, burglaries, domestic violence, and rampant drug dealing and abuse.

Buses and vans pull up; kids rush into the Center, excited voices clamoring and young arms pushing. The after-school program is beginning. Teachers brace for the excess energy of the

The Edna Martin Christian Center.

children and respond with activities ranging from homework tutoring to drug abuse prevention, faith and values lessons, anger management, and tips on respecting the rights of others.

Of course, the children will be fed—home-cooked meatloaf, potatoes, green beans, and other nutritious fares as well as cake. Some of the kids now shun the meal that is still carefully prepared from contributions of food and money; instead, they prefer the promise of a later Big Mac with fries.

Work at the Center early in the new millennium is still a work of faith, perhaps not an "Edna" faith, but a different kind of faith. It is a faith that reaches out to many different organizations and agencies in order to better serve a poor, hurting community in a city praised for progress and prosperity. It is still a faith that changes lives, especially young lives.

American Baptist churches throughout the state continue to send money to support the Center, even though many Baptists who knew Edna Martin personally and felt her magnetism are now gone. If there had been no Edna, there would be little support now. Her faith was the mustard seed.

Edna's painted image looks from a mural in a classroom where the older children gather to participate in planned activities or just hang out. Edna is accompanied on the wall by Dr. Martin Luther King, Jr., Malcolm X, and Michael Jordan. The teenage artist who painted the mural did not know how Edna might feel about her wall companions, and maybe he would not have cared. He had studied black history in school, and Edna was a great one to teach black history,[1] and he knew who the African-American heroes were. He had been given a picture of Edna as the founder of the Center. If left to his discretion, she might not have appeared in the mural at all.

The story of the Edna Martin Christian Center begins with the story of a remarkable woman—a woman who had the faith to venture forth in a strange place where she was not wanted and seek out children in the direst of circumstances to win them for Christ. She believed that the Gospel of Jesus Christ could change lives and communities, and she, along with the help of thousands—black and white—proved God's promises to be true.

There are hundreds of middle-aged to senior men and women living in the Indianapolis community and beyond who remember Edna well. They have one thing in common: if you mention her name, they will smile.

The story does not end with Edna Martin. She would not have wanted that. Her house might have come to be called by her name, but it was never built on her name. It was built on her faith. Now names such as the Martindale-Brightwood Community Development Corporation, the Hillside Neighborhood Organization, the Community Resurrection Partnership, the Tech High School Community Council, the Harshman Junior High Bridges to Success program, the Indianapolis Police Department Citizen Task Force, the Inter-denominational Ministerial Alliance, the Annie E. Casey Foundation City-wide Family Circles program, and the Citizens Multi-

Service Center share the dream.

A new facility also shares the dream. The Edna Martin Outreach Center at Genesis Plaza, a beautiful new facility located at 2855 North Keystone, is a partnership of the Community Centers of Indianapolis and the Edna Martin Christian Center. Most of the programs started by Edna—the after-school program, seniors' program, and teen program—will still operate out of the Caroline Avenue facility. The Outreach Center will initially house a social worker and receptionist and will provide many of the same supports that the Center has provided, along with utility assistance, job training, and other services, such as legal advice. Other programs located at Genesis Plaza are a health center, the neighborhood community development corporation, and several service agencies.

American Baptists oversee the work of the Center as they have faithfully done since 1945. The Center is a nonprofit corporation affiliated with the Board of National Ministries of the American Baptist Churches, USA, one of the most racially diverse of all Protestant denominations. A board of directors composed of persons representing American Baptist churches and the communities that they serve governs the Center. The Edna Martin Christian Center is one of eighteen Neighborhood Action Program centers sponsored by American Baptists across the country from the West Coast to the Mississippi Delta to Rhode Island.

Today the Center's mission statement reads: to move people and communities from hopelessness to a vision of hope, bridging cultural, racial, and economic differences, and to empower them, through our witness, to experience the redemptive love of Jesus Christ and to become participants in the Reign of God.[2]

Director of the Edna Martin Christian Center Larry Lindley, who came to this urban ministry from a prosperous career as a mathematician in a defense industry, has a philosophy of service that sustains him. "A Christian sees every individual as created in God's image and as somebody who Christ died for, and I think that gives individuals a lot more value and significance. . . . Faith is not just a system of belief, but is belief in action. James wrote 'faith by itself, if it has no works, is dead.' I would go one step further and say that faith without action is not faith at all, but a mere intellectual game."[3] Edna would have approved.

In the quiet rooms of the house that faith built on Caroline Avenue, in the hours after all the children have gone, families have been given food, the faithful staff and volunteers are heading home—the memory of Edna is there. She is leading the little children gathered around her feet in a familiar chorus, her hands gently moving with the rhythm, her sweet smile encouraging participation, her quiet voice rising and falling with the words.

The foolish man built his house upon the sand,
The foolish man built his house upon the sand,
The foolish man built his house upon the sand,
And the walls came tumbling down.

The walls came down and the floods came up,
The walls came down and the floods came up,
The walls came down and the floods came up,
And the house on the sand went "boom."

The wise man built his house upon the rock,
The wise man built his house upon the rock,
The wise man built his house upon the rock,
And the house on the rock stood firm.[4]

Appendix 1: Speech to Riverside Church, New York City

New York City. 1962

To the Mistress of Ceremonies, the Pastor, officers and members of this congregation, I am delighted to share in this service today— Woman's Day and I certainly feel humble that I have been selected to be your first speaker for this occasion.

I wish to express my deep gratitude to your committee for this lovely corsage I am wearing also.

I have selected for our thinking the subject—Who Cares?

You and I are living in a world of confusion today that is so vast that it is unbelievable. The foundations of our former existence are crumbling all about us. Our leaders are confused and are dreadfully fearful; and yet there was never a time in civilization when we have had so much, rich beyond any other generation.

The great forces of the world have as their ultimate goal the conquering of space beyond the earth, and men have made up their mind to travel to the moon.

Yet we are witnessing a squandering and misuse of not only our money but our time and our talents.

Men and women, boys and girls, have become prisoners of this age and have gradually, but surely, put their material life above their spiritual life.

And we have come to believe that we can be successful, if we are capable, without God. So we have dismissed Him. And we find ourselves in a dreadful calamity, and our world crisis gets worse day by day.

The blazing headlines—the screaming commentators—the shrieking sirens night and day—bullet ridden bodies—mobs—race riots—violence and murder of every kind confronts us.

We are witnessing parents being beheaded and shot because they disagree with their own children. Crimes of every kind are being committed.

I just read an article recently where it stated that in one city alone, there were 3,000 girls plus an estimated 8,000 boys who are members of some gang.

The article stated that these girls presented the same grave problems as the boy gangs. They carried concealed weapons. They offered their bodies as prostitutes in order to obtain money to buy narcotics for the boys.

We are all aware that ten years back we seldom heard of girls committing crimes—but now they are a part of shop lifting, snatching pocket books, holdups, and you can find plenty in the streets any hour of the night, even joining in bank robberies.

We have a murder every 48 minutes, a rape every 34 minutes, an aggregated assault every 4 minutes, a burglary every 30 seconds and a car theft every 2 minutes.

With these honest facts staring us in the face, the question that arises in my mind is where are the hands that rock the cradle?

What has become of mothers who were interested in being at home nights with their family and seeing to it that the homework is done before the radio or television is turned on?

Families used to sit down to the table together. They had times to eat together—large families. This is gone today. Families come in and eat one at a time.

And it is surprising to see how much shopping is done on Sunday now. Not only do the groceries do big business, but the laundry mats are going full swing.

You know children learn by example. We should take our children to church, and set an example.

Do we smoke and drink before our children?

Our children are the richest of all blessings. We should help them to develop themselves and help them to find outlets in the right way.

Then we should teach our children to work. Permit them the satisfaction of personal achievement. We just can't afford to hand them everything on a silver platter.

We have been caught up by these times, and we are substituting material things for spiritual values, and we are in the midst of an unhappy state when we could have Faith and Hope and Love.

May I remind you of a portion of scripture that we are all familiar with. It is found in the 24th Psalm.

"The earth is the Lord's and the fullness there of and all those that dwell therein."

I am happy this morning because I know that God still owns this universe and He is our Heavenly Father.

It was His Hand that hung the world in space, it was His hand that fashioned the flowers of the field. God made the sea and the ocean. It was God who filled this old earth with beauty and the air with a song.

No matter what comes and goes, we must reckon with God.

Gun powder, armed ships, airplanes, submarines and missiles, these are not the weapons we need today.

The challenge to each of us in these trying times is to put away lip service and all shallow worship, because if we are to be useful Christians, ours must be a spiritual strength that comes from really knowing and understanding of God.

We must become new persons in our relationship to prayer. New persons in our appreciation of things that are good and beautiful.

There just must be a distinction between a Christian and an unsaved person. Society is looking for a difference. Mark it down that as soon as an individual uses the same loose language, lives the same kind of life, frequents the same worldly places as does the so-called sinner, one so crooked in his dealings with his fellowmen, his influence as a Christian is gone.

As we look at the world today and see all its defects, the true Christian should not become depressed or discouraged. We should not retreat to helplessness or a lower level of living.

All these things should challenge us to help build a new social order.

I am just back from Kalamazoo College where we held our conference and some of the things that we dwelt upon were the need for a healing ministry.

We have a great population explosion in our country, which will continue. It was predicted that in 1975 we would have 176,000,000 people but today in 1962 we have 180 million.

There will be more forced leisure time. There is a movement on foot now to set the retirement age at 40 years. With increasing population there will be fewer jobs. There will be the permanently unemployed. Juvenile unrest and family breakdown will increase.

In this setting, God is depending upon the Christian and his healing ministry.

In the 30th Chapter of the book of Isaiah, it reads, "In quietness and in confidence shall be our strength."

The quietness that nurtures the soul—the opportunity of prayer, to be still and listen to God, and remember His voice is not the "routine" of life. It is something for which we must strive.

In quietness and confidence shall be our strength.

Our souls are refreshed with the Holy Spirit.

No more ugly thoughts.

Doubts and fears banish.

No more criticism and bitterness.

Only as we are hid in Christ do we really grow.

Let us be confident and remember that if we can trust Him with the affairs of the Universe, we can trust Him with our little lives.

We must care.

There is so much need, so much loneliness.

We must hear the voice of the world's anguished and throbbing hordes.

We must find time to comfort the lonely, give the cup of cold water to those that are thirsty, and tell the blessed story to those who have lost their way—regardless of race or creed, rich or poor.

We need deeper concerns—brotherly love, a feeling of compassion and understanding. Every longing of our souls and every need of our lives are fulfilled when we lay our all on the altar.

So in conclusion, may I suggest that every morning, lean thy arm awhile upon the window sill of Heaven and gaze upon thy God. Then with that vision in your heart, turn to meet the problems of the day.

Gracious Lord, why do we fret or worry when we know that Thou art in control, that Thy will is good, acceptable and perfect.

Forgive us, we pray for ever feeling the slightest concern.

In Jesus' name, Amen.

Appendix 2: Support for East Side Christian Center Reaches New High

Church giving to the ministry of the East Side Christian Center reached a new high in 1969—$22,859.03. One hundred eighty-nine American Baptist churches and 19 churches of other denominations contributed to the program of the Center.

Mrs. Edna M. Martin, director, the staff and board members all want you to know how thankful they are for this encouraging support. "Thanks, and thanks again for your concern for this vital inner-city ministry."

Each church in the Indiana Baptist Convention is urged to contribute to the Center in order that the witness of Christ can be maintained and enlarged in the inner city of Indianapolis.

Alkman Creek	24.53	Brookfield	2.00
Alexandria, First	229.30	Brookston, Federated	20.00
Amo	200.00	Brownstown	10.00
Anderson, First	715.00	Bunker Hill	10.00
Auburn, First	5.00	Calvary, Indianapolis	319.23
Bedford, First	335.00	Camden, First	20.00
Bethany	72.00	Central, Indianapolis	480.00
Bethel, Coffee Creek	55.00	Chrisney	5.00
Bethel, Friendship	60.00	Clayton, First	25.00
Bethlehem	20.36	Clearspring	14.22
Bicknell, First	20.00	Clinton, First	97.87
Big Walnut	15.00	Coalmont	15.00
Bluffton, First	396.00	Coffee Creek	10.00
Brazil	100.00	Columbia City, First	6.00

Connersville, First	100.00	Lewis Creek	220.00
Covenant, Indianapolis	100.00	Liberty, Greensburg	27.42
Crawfordsville, East	924.41	Liberty Center	412.41
Crooked Creek, Indianapolis	333.40	Linton, First	60.00
Crothersville, First	17.83	Logansport Baptist Temple	51.30
Cumberland, First	41.00	Lynhurst, Indianapolis	305.00
Curry's Prairie Union	54.48	Macedonia	18.00
Dabney	20.00	Madison	9.00
Dana	310.00	Marion, First	150.00
Decatur, First	290.00	Martinsville, First	20.00
Dugger, First	15.00	Meadowbrook, Anderson	5.00
Dunkirk	247.06	Memorial Fort Wayne	50.00
Eastern Heights, Evansville	43.30	Metea	4.50
Edwardsport	20.00	Mexico	51.00
Ellettsville	154.24	Miami	10.00
Elwood, First	344.25	Milan, First	480.00
Emerson Avenue, Indianapolis	5.00	Mill Creek	36.24
Emmanuel, Indianapolis	300.00	Mitchell, First	35.00
Emmanuel, Jeffersonville	10.00	Monon, First	39.00
Englewood, Bedford	20.00	Montpelier, First	118.00
Evansville, First	5.00	Morocco United	487.01
Flat Rock Women's Association	25.00	Mounds, Anderson	200.00
Flora	14.50	Mud Pike	15.00
Fort Wayne, First	71.51	Muncie, First	10.00
Frankfort	155.15	Mt. Aerie	5.00
Franklin, First	905.00	Mt. Gilead, Flat Rock	65.00
Freedom	45.79	Mt. Horeb	10.00
Friendly Grove	30.00	Mt. Moriah	125.05
Galveston	100.00	Mt. Olivet	15.00
Garfield Park, Indianapolis	790.00	Mt. Pleasant, Indianapolis	120.00
Garrett, First	93.33	Mt. Pleasant, Orleans	19.20
Gosport	346.10	Mt. Vernon	39.01
Graham	17.50	Mt. Zion, Indianapolis	120.00
Greensburg, First	344.39	New Bethel, Indianapolis	64.42
Hebron	172.11	New Castle, First	10.00
Hills	20.00	New Little Flat Rock	28.49
Hopewell	50.00	New Market	15.00
Huntington, First	28.00	North Madison	5.00
Indianapolis, First	770.70	North Terre Haute	100.00
Jasonville, First	50.00	North Vernon	33.00
Jeffersonville, First	5.00	Oak Grove	46.75
Judson, Indianapolis	35.61	Oak Park, Indianapolis	23.02
Kendallville	10.00	Oolitic	17.35
Lafayette, First	135.00	Oregon	11.50
LaPorte, First	100.00	Osgood	50.00
Laughery Assoc. Golden Age	11.16	Parr	30.00
Lawrenceburg, First	125.00	Peru, First	60.00
Lebanon, Indianapolis	495.00	Plainfield, First	61.00
Lebanon, Linton	5.00	Pleasant View, Flat Rock	602.00

Poneto	90.00	Young America	38.89
Quincy	60.00	Zion	12.00
Richmond, First	100.00	Zion's Hill	25.00
Rochester, First	75.00		
Rock Creek	61.65	**Other Church Gifts:**	
Rockville	3.00	Brightwood United Methodist	25.00
Rosedale	16.00	Brookside United Methodist	97.00
Rushville, First	200.00	Centenary Christian	25.00
Ryker's Ridge	5.00	Faith United Church of Christ	68.00
Salem, Bethel	396.07	Church of Galesburg, Illinois	35.00
Salem, Harmony	33.00	Good Samaritan	25.00
Sardinia	50.00	Kingsburg, W. C. S. S.	5.00
Scottsburg, First	250.00	Meridian Heights	12.00
Second, Mt. Pleasant	76.14	Mt. Olive Baptist Church	60.00
Seymour, First	310.00	New Baptist Church	5.00
Shelbyville, First	283.83	New Bethel National	
Sitka	30.00	Conference	100.00
Smith Valley	10.00	New York Street	
Spice Valley	30.00	United Methodist	5.00
Southport, Indianapolis	545.00	Second Missionary, Terre Haute	50.00
Star	40.00	South Calvary	10.00
Sullivan	676.82	Third Christian Church	1.00
Summitville, First	220.00	Woodruff Place Christian	
Tanglewood	50.00	Service League	50.00
Tell City	87.00	Anonymous Church	71.87
Tennessee Valley	29.50	**Total:**	**$22,859.03**
Terre Haute, First	300.00		
Tuxedo Park, Indianapolis	420.95		
Union Assoc. Women's Conf.	80.00		
Union Flat Rock, Sand Creek	25.00		
Union, Curry's Prairie	25.00		
Union, Judson	10.00		
Unity	5.00		
Versailles	115.00		
Vincennes	77.81		
Waldron	139.00		
Warren, First	21.73		
Washington, Laughery	27.25		
Washington, Union	47.00		
Waynetown	128.00		
West Lafayette, Federation	100.00		
Westview, Indianapolis	250.00		
Whitelick Men's Brotherhood	40.00		
Wilson Creek	10.00		
Windfall	10.00		
Wirt	4.00		
Wolcott	25.00		
Woodland	120.00		
Woodruff Place, Indianapolis	358.32		

East Side Christian Center Board
1962

Term Ending 1962
Rev. Stewart H. Silver (1)
Mrs. Donald Learner (1)
Dr. W. O. Breedlove (2)
Mrs. Pearl B. Smith (2)
Dr. A. D. Pinckney (3)
Mrs. W. Owsley (3)
Rev. W. D. Edwards (4)
Mr. J. F. Johnson (4)

Term Ending 1963
Mrs. Julia Burns (1)
Rev. Robert L. Marlett (1)
Rev. Floyd F. Smith (2)
Mr. Ray S. Spencer (2)
Dr. Clinton M. Marsh (3)
Mrs. Leonard Pearson (3)
Mrs. Sarah Zeigler (4)
Rev. William R. Hughley (4)

Term Ending 1964
Rev. Marvin Utter (1)
Mr. Henry Handly (1)
Rev. Paul L. Madinger (2)
Mrs. Edith Moore (2)
Mrs. William N. Guess (3)
Mrs. Clarence B. LaDine (3)
Mr. B. J. Jackson (4)
Rev. Andrew J. Brown (4)

1. Indiana Baptist Convention
2. Indianapolis Baptist Association
3. Community
4. Negro Baptist Churches

Notes

Preface

   1. Martindale/Brightwood Neighborhood, Indianapolis, Indiana, Timeline 1872–1994, *The Project on Religion and Urban Culture,* The Polis Center, IUPUI, June 1999, p. 2.

   2. Emma Lou Thornbrough, "The History of Black Women in Indiana," in *Indiana's African-American Heritage: Essays from* Black History News & Notes, Wilma Gibbs, ed. (Indianapolis: Indiana Historical Society, 1993), 67–68

1. From Kentucky Roots to Indiana River Towns

   1. E. Eric Lincoln and Lawrence H. Mamiya, *The Black Church in the African American Experience* (Durham and London: Duke University Press, 1990), 9.

   2. Darrel E. Bigham, *An Evansville Album: Perspectives on a River City, 1812–1988* (Bloomington: Indiana University Press, 1988), 19.

   3. Crittenden County, Kentucky, marriage records, Indiana State Library, Indianapolis, Ind. Author's Note: A William Barnes and a B. W. Barnes, white landowners, both at times were shown as witnesses or their homes as being the site of a colored wedding. A Miss Allie Barnes married a Sampson Hodge, both colored, at the home of Sally Barnes, the wife of B. W. Barnes.

   4. Marion B. Lucas, *A History of Blacks in Kentucky*, vol. 1, *From*

Slavery to Segregation, 1760–1891 (Lexington: The Kentucky Historical Society, 1992), 291.

5. Ibid., 327.

6. Ibid., 195, 182.

7. 1910 Census Index: Indiana, *Generations by Heritage Quest* CD, Genealogy Division, Indiana State Library.

8. Marvin E. Harvey, "Blacks in Livingston County, Kentucky," in *Livingston County, Kentucky*, vol. 1, *History and Families, 1798–1989* (Paducah, Ky.: Turner Publishing Co., 1989), 57, quoting Professor Joel Williamson's study.

9. Lucas, *From Slavery to Segregation*, 257–58.

10. Darrel E. Bigham, *Towns and Villages of the Lower Ohio* (Lexington: The University Press of Kentucky, 1998), 232.

11. Ibid., 231.

12. Karen Bridges research, Edna Martin Christian Center Archives, Indianapolis, Ind. (hereafter cited as EMCCA).

13. Harvey, "Blacks in Livingston County," 60.

14. Ibid., 68.

15. Thelma Herrington, interview with Karen Bridges, 11 June 1990, EMCCA.

16. Edna Barnes Birth Record, Posey County Birth Records, September 1893–June 1900, Mount Vernon, Indiana.

17. Bigham, *Towns and Villages of the Lower Ohio*, 251.

18. Ibid., 170.

19. *Indianapolis Recorder*, 20 Sept. 1902.

20. *Mount Vernon Western Star*, 25 Nov. 1897.

21. Ibid.

22. Ibid.

23. Ibid., 10 Aug. 1897.

24. Darrel E. Bigham, *We Ask Only a Fair Trial* (Bloomington: Indiana University Press, in association with the University of Southern Indiana, 1987), 23.

25. *Evansville City Directory*, 1901, p. 91.

26. Ibid., 816.

27. Bigham, *We Ask Only a Fair Trial*, 58.

28. Ibid., 111.

29. Twelfth Census of the United States, Pigeon Township, Vanderburgh County, vol. 76, Enumeration District no. 127, sheet 7,

taken by Fred H. Bixby on 6 June 1900. [Index – B652, Barnes, William].

    30. Bigham, *We Ask Only a Fair Trial*, 34.

    31. Ibid.

    32. Twelfth Census of the United States, Pigeon Township.

    33. City of Evansville Health Department Records, 9 June 1900.

    34. *Indianapolis Journal*, 6–8, 10–11, 20–21 July 1903, and Bigham, *We Ask Only a Fair Trial*, 104–5.

2. Scioto Street and a City Built on Sand

    1. Thelma Barnes, Marion County, Indiana, Birth Records, July 1882 to September 1907.

    2. "The History of Indiana Avenue," Edna Martin Christian Center Archives, Indianapolis, Ind. (hereafter cited as EMCCA).

    3. James H. Madison, *The Indiana Way* (Bloomington and Indianapolis: Indiana University Press and Indiana Historical Society, 1986), 241.

    4. *Indianapolis Star*, 9 May 1999.

    5. Jacob Piatt Dunn, *History of Greater Indianapolis*, 2 vols. (Chicago: The Lewis Publishing Co., 1910), 1:253

    6. Ibid.

    7. *Indianapolis Recorder*, 12 Jan. 1901.

    8. Ibid.

    9. *Indianapolis Recorder*, 1902, newspaper file, EMCCA.

    10. Emma Lou Thornbrough, *Indiana Blacks in the Twentieth Century*, edited and with a final chapter by Lana Ruegamer (Bloomington: Indiana University Press, 2000), 14–15.

    11. *Indianapolis City Directory*, 1904.

    12. Thelma Herrington, interview with Karen Bridges, 11 June 1990, EMCCA.

    13. Indianapolis city directories (1903–1909).

    14. Leon F. Litwack, *Trouble in Mind: Black Southerners in the Age of Jim Crow* (New York: Alfred A. Knopf, 1998), 31–33.

    15. Herrington interview.

    16. James H. Madison, *Eli Lilly: A Life, 1885–1977* (Indianapolis: Indiana Historical Society, 1989), 23.

    17. Ibid., 15.

    18. National Register of Historic Places Continuation Sheet, Section Number 8, page 2, St. Joseph Neighborhood Historic District, United

States Department of the Interior, National Park Service, files of the Historic Landmarks Foundation of Indiana, Indianapolis, Ind.

19. Charlotte Cathcart, *Indianapolis from Our Old Corner* (Indianapolis: Indiana Historical Society, 1965), 24–29.

20. Ibid., 50–58.

21. Ibid., 57. Fourth Presbyterian Church was located on the back of the lot at the northwest corner of Pennsylvania and Pratt Streets.

22. Architectural Highlights of the St. Joseph Historic Neighborhood, n.d., St. Joseph Historic Neighborhood Association, Indianapolis, Indiana.

3. Lessons to Learn

1. Ruth Crocker, "Sympathy and Science: The Settlement Movement in Gary and Indianapolis to 1930" (Ph.D. diss., Purdue University, 1982).

2. David J. Bodenhamer and Robert G. Barrows, eds., *The Encyclopedia of Indianapolis* (Bloomington and Indianapolis: Indiana University Press, 1994), 577.

3. *Indianapolis Star*, 18 June 2000.

4. Ibid.

5. Emma Lou Thornbrough, "The History of Black Women in Indiana," in *Indiana's African-American Heritage: Essays from* Black History News & Notes, Wilma Gibbs, ed. (Indianapolis: Indiana Historical Society, 1993), 70–72.

6. Grand Body of the Sisters of Charity Collection, 1912–1977, M619, Indiana Historical Society Library, Indianapolis, Ind.

7. Thornbrough, "History of Black Women in Indiana," 74.

8. Bodenhamer and Barrows, eds., *Encyclopedia of Indianapolis*, 597.

9. *Indianapolis News*, 15 Nov. 1918.

10. *Indianapolis Star*, 1 Aug. 1909.

11. Ibid.

12. Thornbrough, "History of Black Women in Indiana," 77.

13. Darlene Clark Hine, Elsa Barkley Brown, and Rosalyn Terborg-Penn, eds., *Black Women in America*, 2 vols. (Bloomington: Indiana University Press, 1993), 1:358.

14. Jessie Carney Smith, ed., *Notable Black American Women*, 2 vols. (Detroit: Gale Research, 1992), 1:1186.

15. Thornbrough, "History of Black Women in Indiana," 69.

16. A'Lelia Perry Bundles, *On Her Own Ground: The Life and Times of Madam C. J. Walker* (Philadelphia: Chelsea House Publishers, 1991), 154. Bundles is the great-great-granddaughter of Madam Walker.

17. Emma Lou Thornbrough, *Indiana Blacks in the Twentieth Century*, edited and with a final chapter by Lana Ruegamer (Bloomington: Indiana University Press, 2000), 55, 62.

18. Walter B. Hendrickson, *The Indiana Years, 1903–1941* (Indianapolis: Indiana Historical Society, 1983), 128–29, 131.

19. Mrs. B. J. Jackson, "This Is Your Life" script, 17 Jan. 1954, Edna Martin Christian Center Archives, Indianapolis, Ind. (hereafter cited as EMCCA).

20. Thornbrough, *Indiana Blacks in the Twentieth Century*, 38.

21. Thelma Herrington, interview with Karen Bridges, 11 June 1990, EMCCA.

22. Jackson, "This Is Your Life."

4. Edna's Church: Her Cornerstone

1. Emma Lou Thornbrough, "The History of Black Women in Indiana," in *Indiana's African-American Heritage: Essays from Black History News & Notes*, Wilma Gibbs, ed. (Indianapolis: Indiana Historical Society, 1993), 70.

2. E. Eric Lincoln and Lawrence H. Mamiya, *The Black Church in the African American Experience* (Durham and London: Duke University Press, 1990), 274.

3. Darlene Clark Hine, *When the Truth Is Told: A History of Black Women's Culture and Community in Indiana, 1875–1950* (Indianapolis: National Council of Negro Women, Indianapolis Section, 1981), 21.

4. Thelma Herrington, interview with Gwendolyn Crenshaw, Edna Martin Christian Center Archives, Indianapolis, Ind. (hereafter cited as EMCCA).

5. Thelma Herrington, interview with Karen Bridges, 11 June 1990, EMCCA.

6. Mrs. B. J. Jackson, "This Is Your Life" script, 17 Jan. 1954, ibid.

7. *50 Years of Community Service, 1900–1950, Young Men's Christian Association, The Senate Avenue Branch, 450 North Senate Avenue*, booklet in H. J. Richardson Collection, M472, box 23, folder 21, Indiana Historical Society Library, Indianapolis, Ind.

8. Ibid.

9. "The Church That Dares Because It Cares," *The American Baptist*, May 1970.

10. Herrington interview with Karen Bridges, 11 June 1990, EMCCA.

5. Life in the City and a Song Gone

1. Indianapolis Music Promoters Collection, 1903–1977, M635, box 1, folder 18, Indiana Historical Society Library, Indianapolis, Ind.

2. Thelma Herrington, interview with Karen Bridges, 11 June 1990, Edna Martin Christian Center Archives, Indianapolis, Ind. (hereafter cited as EMCCA).

3. *Indianapolis Star*, 4 Apr. 1999.

4. Edward A. Leary, *Indianapolis: The Story of a City* (Indianapolis: The Bobbs-Merrill Co., 1971), 204.

5. Emma Lou Thornbrough, *Indiana Blacks in the Twentieth Century*, edited and with a final chapter by Lana Ruegamer (Bloomington: Indiana University Press, 2000), 48.

6. *Indianapolis Star*, 23 Oct. 2000.

7. *Indianapolis Freeman*, 26 July 1924.

8. Carolyn Brady, "Indianapolis and the Great Migration, 1900–1920," *Black History News & Notes* 65 (Aug. 1996): 6.

9. *Indianapolis Star*, 23 Oct. 2000.

10. Monroe Little, "Towards a History of the Indianapolis African-American Community, 1821–1980," *Black History News & Notes* 59 (Feb. 1955): 5.

11. W. E. B. Du Bois, *The Souls of Black Folk, Essays and Sketches* (New York: New American Library, 1969), 4.

12. Henry J. Richardson, in H. J. Richardson Collection, M472, box 23, folder 21, Indiana Historical Society Library.

13. *Indianapolis Star*, 23 Oct. 2000.

14. Thornbrough, *Indiana Blacks in the Twentieth Century*, 72.

15. "Thelma Barnes to Represent Young Womanhood in Drama 'Which Road Shall I Take,'" *Indianapolis Recorder*, newspaper file, EMCCA.

16. *Indianapolis Star*, 23 Oct. 2000.

17. Ibid.

18. Doris Martin's death notice in the *Indianapolis Recorder*, 17 Jan. 1937.

19. Thelma Herrington, interview with Gwendolyn Crenshaw, EMCCA.

6. Rejuvenation and Revival

1. *Indianapolis Recorder*, 13 Apr. 1940.

2. *Indiana Baptist Observer*, 2 Nov. 1939.

3. *Indianapolis Recorder*, 20 Apr. 1940.

4. Edwin L. Becker, *From Sovereign to Servant: The Church Federation of Greater Indianapolis, 1912–1987* (Indianapolis: The Church Federation of Greater Indianapolis, 1987).

5. Sharon Stone to Gwendolyn Crenshaw, 12 Aug. 1955, Edna Martin Christian Center Archives, Indianapolis, Ind. (hereafter cited as EMCCA).

6. "Housing in Indianapolis, Report of the Citizens Housing Committee," 1940 (Indiana Division, Indiana State Library, Indianapolis, Ind., mimeographed), 1.

7. Ibid.

8. The *Indianapolis Recorder* included activities of the black community in the Brightwood and Oak Hill (Martindale) area in the 26 January 1901 issue. "We find Jackson Scott, the confectioner in Baltimore Avenue; Lincoln Roper, the grocer in East Twenty fifth street; E. D. Artis, grocery, meat market, feed store and hall in East Twenty-Fifth street; Mr. Broyles, grocery and meat market; Mr. Stallard, the grocer and contractor in Carolina ave. All of them have a lucrative trade from both races."

9. Leon F. Litwack, *Trouble in Mind: Black Southerners in the Age of Jim Crow* (New York: Alfred A. Knopf, 1998), 487.

10. *Indianapolis Recorder*, 30 Jan. 1909. The women were Edna B. Fleming, Ada Morris, Lena Brown, and Lillian Brown.

11. *Indianapolis City Directory*, 1941.

12. Emma Lou Thornbrough, *Indiana Blacks in the Twentieth Century*, edited and with a final chapter by Lana Ruegamer (Bloomington: Indiana University Press, 2000), 27.

13. A kindergarten, nursery, and recreation department at 2626 E. Twenty-fifth Street was opened by Galilee Baptist Church in March 1940, north of the targeted Martindale area. Its purpose, stated in a newspaper notice, was to "stimulate more interest in the community and its children." The executive secretary of the project was Rev. D. B. Dudley. Other instructors were Mrs. Carrie Oldham, George Phillips, and Miss Frances Fletcher. *Indianapolis Recorder*, 16 Mar. 1940.

14. Mrs. B. J. Jackson, "This Is Your Life" script, 17 Jan. 1954,

EMCCA.

15. "'Recollections' of Dr. Martin as Told to Virginia Sutton," *The American Baptist*, Sept. 1974, p. 7.

7. The Winds Shall Not Prevail

1. George Blake, *Finding a Way through the Wilderness: The Indiana Baptist Convention, 1833–1983* (Indianapolis: Central Publishing Co., 1983), 236.

2. Rev. R. T. Andrews, interview, Edna Martin Christian Center Archives, Indianapolis, Ind. (hereafter cited as EMCCA).

3. Eastside Christian Center, slide presentation, EMCCA.

4. "History of the New Bethel Missionary Baptist Church: Cherish the Past, Affirming the Present, Building for the Future, 1875–1990," The Polis Center, IUPUI, File 13 (photograph) and 20.

5. Unpublished biographical sketch, EMCCA.

6. Edna Martin, interview with Rev. Louis Nelson, 1974, ibid.

7. Luke 15:8–10.

8. "'Recollections' of Dr. Martin as Told to Virginia Sutton," *The American Baptist*, July/Aug. 1974.

9. Unpublished biographical sketch, EMCCA.

10. Rosa Lee Brown and Mildred Majors, interview with author, 16 July 2001.

11. Jon Carlstrom, interview with author, 12 Nov. 1999.

12. *Indianapolis News*, 1 Dec. 1967.

13. *The Newsette*, Aug.–Sept. 1947, p. 10.

14. Paraphrase of Luke 24:13–35.

15. Jo Diane Westmoreland Ivey, interview with Gwendolyn Crenshaw, 30 Nov. 1995, EMCCA.

16. *Indianapolis Star*, 16 Nov. 1991.

17. Paraphrase of Genesis chapters 35–47.

18. Joshua Cutler, interview with Karen Bridges, 23 Nov. 1991, EMCCA.

19. Ibid.

20. History of New Bethel Missionary Baptist Church, Indiana Historical Society Library, Indianapolis, Ind.

21. Darlene Clark Hine, Elsa Barkley Brown, and Rosalyn Terborg-Penn, eds., *Black Women in America*, 2 vols. (Bloomington: Indiana University Press, 1993), 1:86.

22. Celestine D. Pettrie, telephone interview with author, 28 May 2001.

8. Solid Faith in a Shaky House

1. *Indianapolis News*, 16 Nov. 1950.

2. Edward A. Leary, *Indianapolis: The Story of a City* (Indianapolis: The Bobbs-Merrill Co., 1971), 208.

3. *Indiana Baptist Observer*, July–Aug. 1974, p. 13.

4. American Baptist Assembly Archives, box 1946, Green Lake, Wisc.

5. Rev. Ralph Beaty, interview with Karen Bridges, 15 Jan. 1993, Edna Martin Christian Center Archives, Indianapolis, Ind. (hereafter cited as EMCCA).

6. Joseph H. Stevens, "Penn Center Historical District, St. Helena Island, South Carolina," Heritage Celebration, November 1999, St. Helena Island, S.C.

7. Carrie Bell Brown, interview with author, Dayton, Ohio, 12 Nov. 1999.

8. East Side Christian Center Board, "Constitution of the Eastside Christian Center," EMCCA.

9. Frank Alexander, interview with author, 4 Nov. 1999.

10. E. Eric Lincoln and Lawrence H. Mamiya, *The Black Church in the African American Experience* (Durham and London: Duke University Press, 1990), 241.

11. Brown interview.

12. Edna Martin, interview, 17 Dec. 1973, EMCCA.

13. Beaty interview.

14. Joshua Cutler, interview with Karen Bridges, 23 Nov. 1991, EMCCA.

15. Beaty interview.

16. Wanda Dunn, Martha Wales, Mary Alice Medlicott, Lynne Schuetz, interview with author, Franklin, Ind., 26 July 2001.

17. Ibid.

18. Ibid.

19. Ibid.

20. Unpublished biographical sketch, EMCCA.

21. Edna Martin, interview, 7 Mar. 1974, ibid.

22. Ibid.

23. East Side Christian Center minutes, 31 Mar. 1958, EMCCA.

24. L. Eugene Ton, interview with author, 9 Nov. 1999.

25. Edna Martin Christian Center Archives.

26. Rosa Lee Brown, interview with author, at home of Mildred Majors, 16 July 2001.

27. East Side Christian Center, "Announcement of Annual Assembly," 1961, EMCCA.

28. Mary Mapes, "Religion and Social Welfare in 20th Century Indianapolis," *Research Notes, from the Project on Religion and Urban Culture*, The Polis Center, IUPUI, June 1999, vol. 2, no. 3, p. 1.

29. Cutler interview.

30. "Celebration of a Dream: Edna Martin Christian Center, 1941–1981," p. 3, EMCCA.

31. Edward D. Rapp, "Study of East Side Christian Center," report, 1957, ibid.

32. *Indianapolis Star*, 7 Aug. 1949.

33. "Christmas Greetings to Friends of the East Side Christian Center," Dec. 1959, EMCCA.

34. Edna Martin interview.

9. Programming Around the Rock

1. Friends of the East Side Christian Center and Friendliness Guild Members, letter of 22 Jan. 1954, Edna Martin Christian Center Archives, Indianapolis, Ind. (hereafter cited as EMCCA).

2. *The East Side Center News*, June 1955, EMCCA.

3. Edna Martin, interview, 17 Dec. 1973, ibid.

4. Unpublished biographical sketch, ibid.

5. Louis Nelson, interview with author, Green Lake, Wisc., 16 Oct. 1999.

6. Edna Martin Christian Center Archives.

7. *The East Side Center News*, June 1955, EMCCA.

8. Mildred Majors, interview with author, 16 July 2001.

9. Ibid.

10. East Side Christian Center, staff for 1959–60, EMCCA.

11. East Side Christian Center Treasurer's Report, Apr. 1958, ibid.

10. Tested and Tried and Found Wanting

1. Mrs. B. J. Jackson, "This Is Your Life" script, 17 Jan. 1954, Edna Martin Christian Center Archives, Indianapolis, Ind. (hereafter cited as EMCCA).

2. Paul Crafton, interview with author, 17 Nov. 1999, and also comments of many others who were in the program.

3. Edward D. Rapp, "Study of East Side Christian Center," report, 1957, EMCCA.

4. Ibid., 11.

5. Ibid., 13.

6. Ibid., 3, 4.

7. Ibid., 13.

8. Marjorie Bell, interview with Gwendolyn Crenshaw, EMCCA.

11. A Closer Look at the Harvest Field

1. Larry Rood, "A Community Study for the East Side Christian Center," Sept. 1962. This is an unpublished research study supported by the East Side Christian Center in cooperation with other public agencies. Edna Martin Christian Center Archives, Indianapolis, Ind.

2. Ibid., 1.

3. Ibid., 3, 4.

4. Ibid., 15.

5. Ibid., 16.

6. Ibid.

7. Ibid., 26.

8. Ibid.

9. Ibid.

12. Rich Men, Good Gifts, and Blind Faith

1. 1967 Report of the East Side Christian Center, Edna Martin Christian Center Archives, Indianapolis, Ind. (hereafter cited as EMCCA).

2. East Side Christian Center Board Minutes, 23 Mar. 1964, EMCCA.

3. Edna Martin Christian Center Archives.

4. Paul Madinger, "The East Side Christian Center <u>Must</u> Have a New Building!," EMCCA.

5. John S. Lynn, telephone interview with author, 6 May 1999.

6. Ibid.

7. James H. Madison, *Eli Lilly: A Life, 1885–1977* (Indianapolis: Indiana Historical Society, 1989), 217.

8. Lilly Endowment, Inc., *Report for 1963*, p. 9, quoted in Madison, *Eli Lilly*, 215.

9. *50 Years of Community Service, 1900–1950, Young Men's Christian Association, The Senate Avenue Branch*, H. J. Richardson Collection, M472, box 23, folder 21, Indiana Historical Society Library, Indianapolis, Ind.

10. John G. Rauch, Sr., to Eli Lilly, 27 May [1964], quoted in Madison, *Eli Lilly*, 234.

11. Madison, *Eli Lilly*, 236.

12. Ibid.

13. Ibid., 237.

14. Ibid., 218.

15. Richard Padrick, interview with author, 7 Nov. 1999.

16. Rev. Ralph Beaty, interview with Karen Bridges, 15 Jan. 1993, EMCCA.

17. Rev. Orville Sutton, telephone interview with author.

18. *The Baptist Observer*, 2 Jan. 1968, p. 7.

19. Beaty interview.

20. Ibid.

13. Work in the House That Faith Built

1. Dedication Program, Edna Martin Christian Center Archives, Indianapolis, Ind. (hereafter cited as EMCCA).

2. Edna Martin, interview, 7 Mar. 1974, ibid.

3. Rev. Ralph Beaty, interview with Karen Bridges, 15 Jan. 1993, ibid.

4. Edna Martin, interview, 17 Dec. 1973, ibid.

5. Unpublished biographical sketch, ibid.

6. Beaty interview.

7. Edna Martin interview, 7 Mar. 1974.

8. Ibid.

9. Larry Rood, "A Community Study," an unpublished research study supported by the East Side Christian Center in cooperation with other public agencies, 1962, EMCCA.

10. Edna Martin, "Do You Teach Religion?," *The Baptist Crusader*, May 1970.

11. Richard Padrick, interview with author, 7 Nov. 1999.

12. East Side Christian Center "Minutes," paper presented at the Board of Directors of East Side Christian Center, 30 Apr. 1962, EMCCA.

13. R. T. Andrews, interview, 1992, ibid.

14. *The Baptist Observer*, 2 Jan. 1968, p. 7.

15. *Indianapolis Star*, 14 July 2001. In this article, Judith Cebula tells

of the impact of Rev. Boniface Hardin, a Benedictine Catholic priest who founded Martin University to serve low-income and nontraditional students in Indianapolis. Martin University is located in the Martindale neighborhood. Hardin, as a young priest, witnessed the impact of the construction of Interstate 65 on Holy Angels parish on the west side of Indianapolis, cutting off a once-vibrant community from the rest of the city. He saw the same situation when Interstate 70 divided the Martindale neighborhood.

14. Winds of Change and Bright, Hip Kids

1. L. Eugene Ton, interview with author, 9 Nov. 1999.
2. Paul Crafton, telephone conversation with author, 3 Aug. 1999.
3. Paul Crafton, letter to author, 20 Jan. 2000.
4. Ibid.
5. Ibid.
6. Paul Crafton, interview with author, 17 Nov. 1999.
7. Marsha Bridwell McDaniel letter, 30 June 1963, Edna Martin Christian Center Archives, Indianapolis, Ind. (hereafter cited as EMCCA).
8. Jon Carlstrom, interview with author, 12 Nov. 1999.
9. Ibid.
10. Rev. Ralph Beaty, interview with Karen Bridges, 15 Jan. 1993, EMCCA.
11. James W. McDaniel, letter to author, 24 July 1999.
12. Ibid.

15. Days of Unrest, the Rock, and Dr. Martin Luther King, Jr.

1. Rev. Ralph Beaty, "Special Issue," East Side Christian Center *News N' Notes*, 1969, Edna Martin Christian Center Archives, Indianapolis, Ind. (hereafter cited as EMCCA).
2. Jon Carlstrom, interview with author, 12 Nov. 1999.
3. Paul Crafton, interview with author, 3 Aug. 1999.
4. Martin Luther King, Jr., *Non-aggression Procedures to Interracial Harmony* (Valley Forge, Penn.: National Ministries, American Baptist Churches USA, 1996), 11.
5. Stanley Warren, "Martin Luther King, Jr. in Indiana," *Black History News & Notes* 73 (Aug. 1998): 3.
6. Emma Lou Thornbrough, *Indiana Blacks in the Twentieth Century*, edited and with a final chapter by Lana Ruegamer (Bloomington: Indiana University Press, 2000), 164.

7. Richard Pierce, "Self-Help in Indianapolis," *Black History News & Notes* 60 (May 1995): 6.

8. Thornbrough, *Indiana Blacks in the Twentieth Century*, 34.

9. Celestine D. Pettrie, telephone interview with author, 28 May 2001.

10. Greg Stone, "Remembering Black Indianapolis," *Indiana Folklore and Oral History* 14, no. 1 (1985): 39.

11. Rosa Lee Brown, interview with author, 16 July 2001.

12. Ibid.

13. *Indianapolis News*, 12 Apr. 1965.

14. Pierce, "Self-Help in Indianapolis," 5.

15. Roundtable, *Research Notes, from the Project on Religion and Urban Culture,* The Polis Center, IUPUI, Sept. 2000, vol. 2, no. 9, p. 6.

16. Robert Franklin, "The Safest Place on Earth: The Culture of Black Congregations," ibid.

17. Elfriede Wedam, "The Mosaic of Black Religion in Indianapolis," ibid., 2.

18. Edna Martin letter, n.d., EMCCA.

16. The Line in the Sand, Hidden Tears, and Edna's Manifesto

1. Frank Alexander, interview with author, 4 Nov. 1999.

2. *The Baptist Observer*, 7 July 1964.

3. Richard Padrick, interview with author, 7 Nov. 1999.

4. L. Eugene Ton, interview with author, 9 Nov. 1999.

5. Paul Crafton, interview with author, 17 Nov. 1999.

6. Richard Pierce, "Self-Help in Indianapolis," *Black History News & Notes* 60 (May 1995): 4.

7. Ibid.

8. *Indianapolis Recorder*, 9 Apr. 1966.

9. Jon Carlstrom, interview with author, 17 Nov. 1999.

10. *Indianapolis Star*, 7 Mar. 1999.

11. Ibid., 21 Apr. 1968.

12. Carlstrom interview.

13. Interviews with Martin family, Karen Bridges 1990, Edna Martin Christian Center Archives, Indianapolis, Ind. (hereafter cited as EMCCA).

14. Celestine D. Pettrie, telephone interview with author, 28 May 2001.

15. James Robert Martin, interview with author, 29 May 2001.

16. *Indianapolis Star*, 28 July 1969.

17. Carlstrom interview.

18. James W. McDaniel, memo to author, 15 Feb. 2000.

19. Carlstrom interview.

20. Crafton interview.

21. Stephen C. Rose, "Putting It to the Churches, Reparations for Blacks?," *The New Republic*, 21 June 1969, p. 20.

22. James Forman, "Black Manifesto," National Black Economic Development Conference, EMCCA.

23. *The Baptist Observer*, 1 July 1969.

24. Ibid.

25. Edna Martin, East Side Christian Center *News N' Notes*, July 1969, EMCCA.

26. Ibid.

27. *The American Baptist*, Nov. 1970.

28. East Side Christian Center *News N' Notes*, Feb. 1969, EMCCA.

17. Family Shelter in the Time of Storm

1. *Indianapolis Times*, 16 Jan. 1954.

2. Paul Crafton, interview with author, 17 Nov. 1999.

3. James Robert Martin, interview with author, 29 May 2001.

4. Darrell Richard Martin, interview with Karen Bridges, 1992, Edna Martin Christian Center Archives, Indianapolis, Ind. (hereafter cited as EMCCA).

5. Brenda Martin Wilcox, interview with author, 30 May 2001, and James Robert Martin, interview with author, 29 May 2001.

6. Darrell Richard Martin interview.

7. James Robert Martin interview with Karen Bridges, 12 Oct. 1990, EMCCA.

8. Wilcox interview.

9. Ibid.

10. Ibid.

11. Darrell Richard Martin interview.

18. Earthly Awards, Heavenly Rewards

1. Jessie Carney Smith, ed., *Notable Black American Women*, 2 vols. (Detroit: Gale Research, 1992), 1:69.

2. Ibid., 2:579.

3. Darlene Clark Hine, *When the Truth Is Told: A History of Black Women's Culture and Community in Indiana, 1875–1950* (Indianapolis: National Council of Negro Women, Indianapolis Section, 1981).

4. Darlene Clark Hine, "Contributions of Black Men and Women in Indiana History," presentation delivered at *Indianapolis Recorder* Women's Charities, Indianapolis, Ind., 5 May 1984, M472, box 24, folder 12, p. 5, Indiana Historical Society Library, Indianapolis, Ind.

5. Rev. Ralph Beaty, interview with Karen Bridges, 1993, Edna Martin Christian Center Archives, Indianapolis, Ind. (hereafter cited as EMCCA).

6. *The Baptist Observer*, n.d., EMCCA.

7. Leon F. Litwack, *Trouble in Mind: Black Southerners in the Age of Jim Crow* (New York: Alfred A. Knopf, 1998), 376.

8. *Indianapolis Star*, 24 Apr. 1971.

9. *Indianapolis News*, 13 June 1979.

10. *Indianapolis Star*, 1972, newspaper files, EMCCA.

11. Howard Thurman, Poem, quoted by Edna Martin, East Side Christian Center *News N' Notes*, Mar. 1970, ibid.

19. Last Days and the Thief in the Night

1. Edna Martin, interview, 7 Mar. 1974, Edna Martin Christian Center Archives, Indianapolis, Ind. (hereafter cited as EMCCA).

2. Edna Martin, interview, 17 Dec. 1973, EMCCA.

3. *The Baptist Crusader*, Feb. 1970.

4. East Side Christian Center *News N' Notes*, Mar. 1970, EMCCA.

5. Ibid.

6. Ibid.

7. Jon Carlstrom, interview with author, 21 June 2000.

8. *The Baptist Crusader*, Jan. 1970.

9. *The American Baptist*, Feb. 1974.

10. Brenda Wilcox, interview with author, 30 May 2001.

11. Rev. Ralph Beaty, interview with Karen Bridges, 1993, EMCCA.

12. Celestine D. Pettrie, telephone interview with author, 28 May 2001.

13. Wilcox interview.

14. Edna Martin, letter to Earl Martin, Jr., EMCCA.

15. Wilcox interview.

16. Ibid.

20. Sister of the Solid Rock

1. Dadashinarehema (Jeanette) Jones, interview with author, 24 July 1999.

2. Ibid.

3. *The American Baptist*, July–Aug. 1974.

4. Frank Alexander, interview with author, 4 Nov. 1999.

5. Tonya Bolden, *And Not Afraid to Dare: The Stories of Ten African-American Women* (New York: Scholastic Press, 1998), 96–106.

6. Ibid.

Epilogue: The Legacy of Edna Martin

1. Jon Carlstrom, interview with author, 12 Nov. 1999.

2. Statement of Ministries, Support, and Mission, Edna Martin Christian Center, Indianapolis, Ind.

3. *Voices of Faith: Making a Difference in Urban Neighborhoods* (Indianapolis: The Polis Center, 1998), 56.

4. "The Wise Man Built His House Upon the Rock," chorus to "The Solid Rock," copyrighted in 1976 by Paragon Associates, Inc., Nashville, Tennessee.

Index